Mompedia

Under the series of Secret Purple Diary

Archana Vashistha

INDIA • SINGAPORE • MALAYSIA

Disclaimer

The information contained in this book is intended to motivate people. The information given in this book is on how you may change and uplift your parenting style. The content in this book is based only on different experiences. All characters and events in this book – even those based on real people – are chosen with their consent.

My intension is clear and pure; I don't want to hurt anyone. So please read this book with an open heart and mind.

The author and the publisher are in no way liable for any dispute. Just be positive and spread positivity around you.

Thanks, and regards

This Book Is Dedicated To

My Grandfather

Lt. Mr. Chaitanya Lal Sharma

(Who always taught us to be independent and self-motivated. He used to write Hindi poems about relations and spirituality)

My Grandmother

Lt. Mrs. Kamla Sharma

(Who is the real inspiration for everyone, a perfect blend of traditions and modern thinking with the courage to stand against pre-defined old regimes)

My Nani ji

Lt. Mrs. Sita Moudgil

&

Lt. Mrs. Leelawati Sharma

(They both were truly dedicated homemakers yet inclined towards spirituality. Their attitude towards life and their experiences in life taught us so many things)

Thanks a lot for inspiring us forever…

This book is dedicated to every woman. You are doing awesome job as daughter, friend, sister, wife, daughter- in- law, mother, educator.

"Remember you are perfectly imperfect"

"keep doing the wonders everyday"

Contents

Acknowledgements

This book would not have been possible without the support of Notion Press Publishers.

I express my heartfelt thankyou to Vasudevan, Yamuna Devi, Swarna Lakshmi, Shanmuga Priya, Rasika Ravindran for crafting this book with their Specialized skills in language editing & making it a beautiful read.

To Notion Press Team From the writing fraternity for encouraging me to express my thoughts freely.

About the Book

In a world where motherhood is an evolving journey filled with joys and challenges, author Archana Vashistha delves into the shifting dynamics of parenthood. Through extensive research, including formal and informal interviews, observations, and conversations with countless mothers across the globe, she presents "Mompedia – under the series of Secret Purple Diary of today's Moms."

Motherhood brings lots of happiness and challenges in a woman's life. Time is changing, society is changing, kids are changing, parenting style is changing, we as Moms are changing.

Now, the big question is why everything is changing so fast? Let's find out the answer of many unanswered questions.

The book aims to empower mothers by enhancing their understanding of their own parenting styles and relationships after getting the Tag MOM. The author celebrates the uniqueness of every child and every mother. She emphasizes the value of self-awareness before adopting any prescribed parenting approach. Join her mission, Purple, to spread awareness of mental health among all age groups, especially women, because only a healthy Mom can raise healthy children. Society may label us, but only fellow mothers truly understand our experiences.

This book is not only about Today's Mom but this tiny little miracle holds **4 generations together- Generation X -** The grandmoms, **generation Y-** The 80% of moms, **generation Z –** The new moms & the young adults and ofcours **The Generation Alpha** , which we all are handelling today.

This book is a collective voice from countless mothers to all mothers out there.

Foreword

In the grand tapestry of family life, mothers are the irreplaceable threads that weave love, warmth, and resilience into the fabric of our existence. They are the silent heroes whose unwavering devotion and boundless strength form the foundation upon which we build our lives.

In this heartfelt tribute to mothers, Author Archana Vashistha is embarking on a journey to honor and celebrate the remarkable women who shape our world with their wisdom, compassion, and unconditional love. From the tender embrace of a mother's arms to the guiding light of her unwavering support, each page of this book is a testament to the profound impact mothers have on our lives.

Through the stories shared within these pages are a glimpse of the extraordinary sacrifice's mothers make, the countless challenges they overcome, and the immeasurable joy they bring into our lives. Whether comforting us in times of sorrow, cheering us on in moments of triumph, or simply being there to listen, mothers are the steadfast pillars of strength upon which we lean.

As we turn the pages of this book, let us pause to reflect on the countless ways in which mothers shape our world, inspire our hearts, and leave an indelible mark on our souls. May this collection serve as a tribute to the boundless love and unwavering devotion of mothers everywhere, reminding us of the immeasurable impact they have on our lives each and every day.

To all the Moms who have poured their hearts and souls into nurturing, guiding, and loving their children, this book is dedicated to you. Your love is the truest and most enduring gift, and your legacy will forever live on in the hearts of those you have touched. "Best of Luck."

With heartfelt gratitude and admiration, many variants of mom.

– Suman Vashistha

Gurugram University- Deputy Registrar, OSD to Vice Chancellor and Director- Industrial Relations & Corporate Affairs

1| Preface - Fun Fact

(The Story behind writing Mompedia)

The reason I started thinking & finally wrote Mompedia is really funny – Once, at a party, I heard the term helicopter mom; I wondered why & how, then someone said she is a social butterfly mom, that's a tiger mom, oh no she is a careless mom, now the hippie mom arrived, oh that's the perfect mom….. bla… bla…. bla…… I was so confused, I remained quiet and started observing everyone, frankly talking I belongs to generation Y the so-called Millennials – I never knew there were so many variants of

Mom.

Previously, I knew only two kinds of Moms: traditional mom (strict) and modern (liberal) later when we grew up working or non-working mom. so, these were the only term we were aware from. But Tiger, hippie, helicopter, shy, influencer, encyclopedia, experimental, in fact wine Mom….. these were not in my dictionary, So, I dogged myself into the theory of different moms, I was curious to know what kind of other terms are popular for Moms?

I decided to research….. google research….. & Instagram research….. & Facebook research…… but those were idealistic, then I decided to do my type of research…….. the real time conversation with thousands of moms.

Throughout my quest to uncover Mom's theory, I encountered numerous mothers spanning different generations, each with their own approaches and outcomes. The conundrum lies in the fact that no one knows the exact formula for being the perfect mom; everyone is navigating the balance. Just as every coin has two sides, every concept has two different approaches. Let's explore further.

Mompedia is not just the production of 1 or 2 months, it's the hard work of many years, numerous of formal informal interviews, observations, experiments, questioners. **It's not just my voice it's the global voice – compiled and curated for all of us.**

2| Meaning of Mom

According to The Oxford Dictionary, the modern word 'mother' is Germanic in origin. It derives from 'moder,' which became 'mutter' in German and 'mōdor' in English. If we go further back, the Germanic 'moder' comes from the Greek 'mētēr' (meaning womb), which in Latin became 'māter.' In India, we call our mother by different names according to religion and place, e.g., Maa, mumma, mummy, Ammi, bebe, amma, mai, etc. But in this book, I'll call all the mothers MOM because I feel a sense of belonging with this word.

A mom is the heart of the family, the one who holds it all together with her unwavering love and strength. She deserves to feel special every day. Mom's mission in life is to make you feel "Amazing." When women have children, they become Moms. They might be a boy mom, a girl mom, a twin mom, or a mom of both. It seems pretty simple. It's the little things that determine the type of mom you'll become and the parenting style you'll use. But, in reality, the only opinions that matter are those. These women are aunts, godmothers, co-workers, friends or neighbors. In my opinion, you don't have to be an actual mom, to be a mother figure to someone.

While exploring the different points of view of Moms from different generations, I can clearly state that balancing the demands of modern motherhood is a tough job. Between kids, work obligations, social commitments, and household duties, trying to fit in a little me time or let alone a date night, balance can seem practically impossible. When Moms do well at work, they feel like they're failing at home, and when they focus on their family, they feel like they're falling behind at work.

A mom who is trying to balance working from home and growing gracefully into this role as a mother, Actually the perfectly imperfect mom is my ideal mom. With the flavor of personal insights and stories to show us how to design a life of your dreams without sacrificing the most important things. Here are the practical advice and fresh ideas.

This book is not about a group of Moms but this book is holding four generations together and giving you all a practical based advice. I request you to recommend this book to every mom and in fact everyone, who wants to know the feeling of Moms because woman truly run the world, but we need a little encouragement along the way.

According to me, "Motherhood is nor the bed of roses or the path of thorns, it's basically the cycle of changing season."

3 | What are the Different Generations?

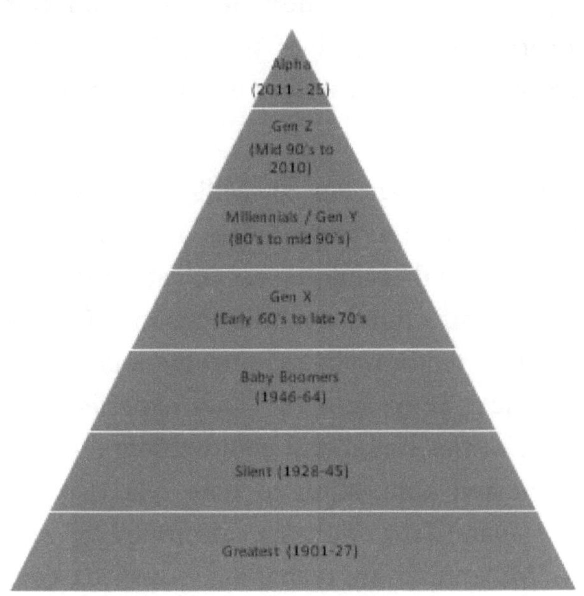

Here is a bit of an introduction about it all, starting with baby boomers**Baby boomers** are typically defined as individuals born between 1946 and 1964 following World War II. They represent a significant demographic cohort known for their large numbers and cultural influence. Baby boomers experienced significant societal changes, including the civil rights movement, the Vietnam War, freedom from British rule and the rise of television and mass media.

They are often associated with values such as hard work, traditional family structures, and economic prosperity. As baby boomers age, they are impacting various aspects of society, including retirement trends, healthcare systems, and consumer markets.

Generation X, born roughly between 1960s and 1980s, is known for its independent and adaptable nature. Growing up during times of economic uncertainty, they witnessed the rise of technology and cultural shifts. Many Gen Xers experienced dual-income households and greater independence at a young age. Gen Xers are currently navigating responsibilities, such as retirement, caregiving for both children and their grandchildren, financial planning for retirement. They are self-sufficient, resourceful, and individualistic, and they have been accustomed to caring for themselves since before reaching adulthood. They value freedom and responsibility and try to overcome challenges on their own.

Generation Y, also known as Millennials, typically refers to individuals born between the early 1980s and mid-1990s. They grew up during a time of rapid technological advancement, witnessing the rise of the internet and digital communication. Millennials are often characterized by their tech-savviness, entrepreneurial spirit, and desire for work-life balance. They tend to value experiences over material possessions and priorities social and environmental causes. Millennials are the most educated generation to date, yet they face challenges such as student loan debt, housing affordability, and job market competitiveness. Millennials are reshaping industries, consumer trends, and workplace culture.

Generation Z, also known as Gen Z, refers to individuals born roughly between the mid-1990s and early 2010s. They are the first generation to grow up entirely in the digital age, surrounded by smartphones, social media, and constant connectivity. Gen Z is characterized by its diversity, technological fluency, and global perspective. They are often described as pragmatic, socially conscious, and inclusive. Growing up in a time of economic uncertainty and social upheaval, Gen Z is passionate about issues such as climate change, racial and gender equality, and mental health awareness. They are also known for their entrepreneurial spirit and preference for authentic, personalized experiences. As Gen Z enters adulthood, they are expected to continue shaping and influencing societal norms, consumer behavior, and workplace dynamics.

Generation Alpha refers to the cohort of individuals born from the early 2010s onwards. As the children of Millennials and Gen Z, they are the first generation to be born entirely in the 21st century. Generation Alpha is growing up in an increasingly digital world, with technology deeply integrated into their daily lives from a very young age. They are expected to be the most technologically adept generation yet, with a natural fluency in digital tools and platforms. Generation Alpha is also growing up in a time of rapid social change and global interconnectedness, which is shaping their values and perspectives. While it's still early to determine all the characteristics of Generation Alpha, they are anticipated to be highly diverse, creative, and globally-minded individuals who will continue to drive innovation and change in the future.

Our Future Generations will be as follows:

- Generation Beta will be born from 2025 to 2039.

- Generation Delta after 2039

According to recent report of **United Nations Population Funds 2024** The world population is around 8 billion strong. Total 65% belongs to age group 15-64 years.

According to the report, India is the most promising country in terms of world economics. We have the most productive population right now. Here are the statistics:

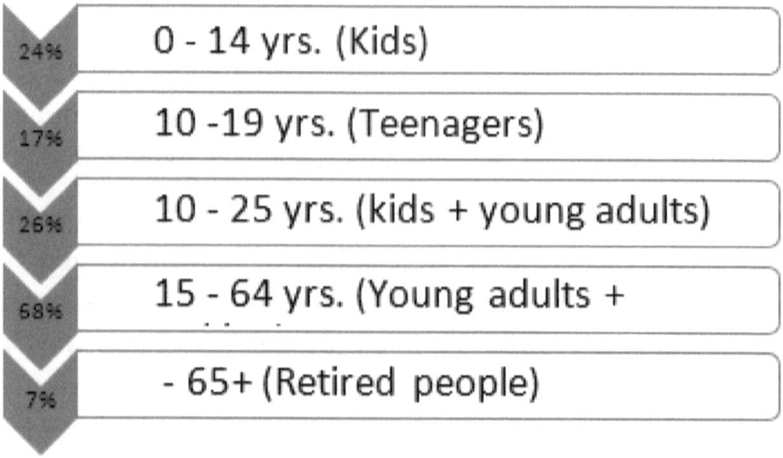

24%	0 - 14 yrs. (Kids)
17%	10 -19 yrs. (Teenagers)
26%	10 - 25 yrs. (kids + young adults)
68%	15 - 64 yrs. (Young adults +
7%	- 65+ (Retired people)

Mompedia represents most of the population, whether kids, Moms, dads or grandparents.

4 | Different Moms - Different Names

The reason I started writing down this book is exploring the different variety of Moms, we all have different choices, values, circumstances and situations. Let's celebrate our uniqueness with the world. We are unapologetically amazing and we are standing together for each other.

1. **The Helicopter Mom** - She hovers, she circles and she swoops in to prevent any perceived danger for her child. This is the mom who is overly involved in her child's growth and development.

2. **The Crunchy Mom** - Urban Dictionary defines a crunchy mom as a Neo-hippie. Neo-hippies are related to a hippie, except that their lives are centered on their kids. People heard this term for the first time on Tik Tok.

3. **The Influencer Mom** - This type of mom is also called a momfluencer. They are known all over social media but mostly target Instagram.

4. **The Glam Mom** - If you're shopping for a "glam mom," someone who loves to look and feel her best, consider gifting her some luxurious skin products or expensive jwellery.

5. **The Shy Mom** - She wants to be included but compared to the previous mom-types she doesn't feel sharing her feelings to others. She passively liking people's posts hoping to be noticed.

6. **The Loner Mom** - She is not here to make friends with other Moms. She prefers sitting away from the group. You can either find her with a book or glued to her mobile.

7. **The Trendy Mom** - She is always up to date with the latest do's and don'ts in parenting, fashion, and lifestyle. She wouldn't be caught dead wearing the wrong color for any event or party.

8. **The Kind Mom** - You won't hear from them unless something negative is happening to her or someone else in the group. She is ready to help anyone without even a single thought.

9. **The Wine Mom** - It's not alcoholism; it's a term that is used to describe a typical upper-middle-class mother, often with young and sophisticated children.

10. **The Magician Mom** - You will know this mom if you find all the children gathered around her, listening to stories or engaging in some creative activity.

11. **The Career Mom** – Super obsessed about her work. She may not attend the kids' PTM or any family function, but she will be on time for her meeting. She is really into her job and does not understand that stay-at-home or part-time working Moms are okay with what they've chosen.

12. **The Bossy Mom** – She knows what's best for her kids and others. It's her way or the highway, no questions asked. This includes questions from other parents as well.

13. **The Gossip Mom** - If she is gossiping with you, you can be sure she is gossiping about you. Her personality is very insecure. She loves to talk, but maybe she's not in the middle of the drama. But she has been the one to tell you all about it and did you hear what so-and-so said about. It's better to beware of her.

14. **The Cool Mom** - She is very popular with her children's friends. Why? Well, when friends come to visit, she treats them and lets them play video games.

15. **The Freestyle Mom** - If you have come across this mom, you would have been shocked to see that she doesn't care if her little ones fall, eat mud or roll in the sand. She says, "Live and let live." This mom believes that children can and should do whatever they like.

16. **The Fitness Mom** - These Moms are sweating it all over social media. They work out, their kids work out, and they post about fitness mantras.

17. **The Perfectionist Mom** - These mothers are controlling, anxious, and deeply care about outward appearances. Their goal is to make their children and family perfect. She is typically an over-controlling, fearful and anxious woman for whom appearance is everything.

18. **The Over-Sharer** - This mom can be a source of information but will likely be the one to spam your mental inbox with too much information.

19. **The Yoga Pants Mom** - This mom drops her kids off at school in full active wear. She's either come from an early morning workout or simply put them on for the late workout.

20. **Breastfeeding Mom** – They are always busy with the little munchkins and tired always. Don't ask them for more coz they are already handling too much. Though breastfeeding obviously has major benefits for mom and baby, it's okay that not all women choose to breastfeed. Don't give them advice without reason.

21. **The By-the-Book Mom** - This is generally not always a first-time mom. She is an experienced mom, and she knows the recommended amount of sleep, food, and chores.

22.**The Humor Mom** - This mom isn't afraid to share "real-life" with every other parent out there. Her posts usually showcase the funny parts of motherhood without any guilt.

23.**The Hover Mom** - Think helicopter mom on steroids. This mother believes that anything and everything in the world outside her door can and will harm her kids, so she protects them like anything.

24.**The Silky Mom** - This type of mom takes a more modern, practical approach to parenthood. These are the opposite of crunchy Moms.

25.**The Religious Mom** – These Moms believe too much in God. Her parenting style combines religious stories, religious food, and religious games.

26.**The Relaxed Mom** - Who believes in peace at home and will do anything to keep things calm and happy. For example, if her daughter spills her bottle of juice, she'll not say a single word, just mop the floor, and that's it, just like nothing happened at all.

27.**Tiger Mom** - This is the type of mom who is super strict, especially when it comes to academics or extracurricular activities. These Moms encourage leadership, independence, and ambition while demonstrating the concepts through their own lives.

28.**The Unpredictable Mom** - These Moms work based on their emotional state at the time. In fact, they don't know how to manage. They are anxious, angry, excessively emotional, and overwhelmed by feelings, so her parenting style is based purely on the situation. There are times when we are all anxious, emotional, moody, and even angry. This is normal as our children grow and life becomes smooth again, but following the same pattern all the time is their way of parenting.

29.**The Pseudo Mom** - She is someone who assumes the role of mom without legally adopting or biologically mothering a child.

This individual, although not a legal mom but she provides everything for the child's needs and typically has a significant emotional bond with the child.

30. **An Unattuned Mom** – She is the one who inserts herself into a baby's space, misreading signals, intruding when the child needs to withdraw; alternatively, an emotionally unavailable mother doesn't respond, teaching the child that she's on her own and needs to self-protect.

31. **The Sigma Mom** - The term "Sigma Mom" has recently emerged in the world of personal development, referring to a mom who is independent, self-sufficient, and highly individualistic.

32. **The Super Mom** - When a mom runs with super energetic power, she feels it in her bones. She is dressed beautifully in clothes that carry no stains. The one who always does everything right and always looks good doing it. She never complains, always smiles, dresses herself and her baby perfectly. Her kids are respectful, and her house is clean. She volunteers for the PTA. She knows to turn playtime into learning time with her toddler.

33. **The Perfect Mom** - It's dependable, charismatic, protective, and energetic, fun loving, happy, responsible, perfect in everything....... Is this kind of mom exist??

34. **No Drama Mama** - In my opinion, these moms are the best. They are my kind of people. Yes, she hears gossip, but she doesn't spread it. She keeps it to herself.

35. **The Complete Mother** - This is the ideal style of mother. However, only approximately 10% of children are lucky enough to have one. This particular mom combines the best elements of all the Moms. They are emotionally balanced, loving, and all-rounder and see their children as individuals and help them

to thrive in all the fields. The loving women moms, who are capable of doing everything with love and without frustration.

After reading about all kinds of Moms, my question is, what kind of mom are you? Ask this question from your child: what kind of mom has he/ she got?

5 | Does Motherhood Change Everything?

All About New Moms

Becoming a Mom is the most precious gift in the world. It's a profound experience that allows an individual to nurture and care for another life, fostering love, growth, and connection. Parenthood can bring immense joy, fulfilment, and a sense of purpose to many individuals, contributing to personal growth and the continuation of family legacy. Society says that No woman is complete without a baby.

Dream of becoming Mom fill us with excitement, but is this all about the good which is going to happen, or does this have another side too, which is – Anxiety, depression during Pregnancy, loneliness, poor self-worth, impact on relationships, tiredness, lack of sleep, struggling with breastfeeding etc.

New Mom Syndrome is also called postpartum blues; the baby blues are actually a mild and temporary form of depression that goes away once hormones level out. Almost every new mother, up to 85 per cent of them, will experience the postpartum blues. You may feel happy one minute and overwhelmed and crying the next.

Their relation with others also changes, some women may feel like they disappear as everyone focuses on the new baby. Mom may feel that her role is simply to care and feed the baby rather than be a partner or person in her own right.

Stress for mothers is often found in multiple and intersecting categories, including how little time Moms have for themselves, shouldering the logistical demands of a household, and often being the family point person for family decisions, big and small. Moms may also struggle with working from home, lack childcare, etc.

What makes her strong is how she continually pushes through the hard days and overcomes challenges to raise her family. Being a parent is one of the most difficult things you'll ever do. It takes courage, sacrifice, strength, and passion.

Dr. Renu Choudhary, Assistant Professor at Law, Gurugram University, shared her experience of early Motherhood.

She explains that a little child requires constant attention, as we know. Motherhood is long, hard and social Obligation and The little child becomes the center of a family hence women feels ignored and helpless which affected her health badly. She further elaborated few points with us:

1. Sleep deprivation and anxiety during pregnancy.

2. Mentally and physically unfit.

3. She can't wear her favorite outfits because of weight gain.

4. Relationship totally changes with the life partner and other family members.

5. Unbearable pain and struggle with breastfeeding.

6. Unwanted Advice from all family members, relatives and neighbors will come from all corners, and everyone seems to be an expert.

Entrepreneur Alka Mahawar shared that as a new mom, I was healing, too. Though there were people around me, I still felt alone.

Sleep-deprived in pain, the days quickly turned into weeks and then months. I wish someone told me before what it would be like to be a mom., every day felt like a hundred years. But today, when I try to think of those days, I don't remember much. It went by so quick.

Mom Blogger and Software Engineer **Prachi Kalra** shared, "Along with the hormonal changes, I went through low self-esteem and postpartum depression as continuous feeding sessions and continuous diaper changing and the same monotonous routine was the most challenging thing for me to deal with. As I am a jolly-natured girl who loves going outside, and someone like me cannot stay-at-home for so long, that was kind of Agni pareeksha for me."

I can't stop sharing the amazingly crafted motherhood journey shared by my friend cum sister by heart, New Mom **Divya Chopra,** What a fun Mom she is, incredible, this is what she shared with me:

- Naam to suna he Hoga - Divya Chopra

- Kaam - "Mere Cement mai Jaan hai" Working Women in Cement Industry as an Assistant Manager in Human Resources.

- Husband- Sidha Sada Banda - Ankit Chopra(What a Busy Man)

- Putr- Bhagwan ka Daan, Mera beta Mridhan, shaitani uska kaam, aur Naani uski jaan.

Being a Mom, life waise he hai, aag ka Dariya hai, Tair kar jana hai... but Diaper, baby feeder aur toys sath lekar jana hai....

- Shaitaniya uski pyaari hai, but some time hum par bhari hai

- Ab tak mobile ke Pro version, sune thai.. ye humara hai

- last movie yaad nhi kab dekhi thi.. ab Toa Masha or Cocomelon ka Jamana hai

- Office se thak Haar kar aane par, iski shaitaniyo ne hi saari thakan bhagana hai

- jitne maa baap sidhei hai, utna mera laal shyana hai

- Bhagwan Har couple ko parents banana, taki unko pata to chale… ki unke parents ne unhe kaise paala hai

- Jitna iska diaper ka ek mahine ka kharcha hai,

  utna mera 2 saal mai saloon ka bill aaya hai

- Bus behan, ye dil se bahar aaya hai, kya batau… kya kehar Dhaya hai

  Isn't she is fabolus, amazingly crafted,

I also answered her in her unique style ;

"Dear till now no one has written like this,

Your writing skills are kamal,

mujhe lagta hai macha dega ye bawal;

Abhi tak sab boring that, ideological baaton ki thi bharmar,

Ab aya kuch dil se nikalkar , devi ji aapko baarambaar pranam.

Are you also smiling after reading this ?

My purpose truly solved…… Coz I wanted to see a smile on your face "My Perfectly Imperfect Mom" You are doing amazing work, keep exploring new horizons every day.

6 | The Best and Worst Parts of Motherhood

Our research defines mothering in many ways, but most include the idea that nurturing children is the central task. Nurturing includes meeting children's physical demands, such as food, clothing, and protection, and it includes loving, cherishing, educating, and training them.

- Delhi-based **Seema Arora**, who is a teacher, social worker and the mom of a special child explained, "The best part about being a mom is unconditional love." She says there isn't any worst part about motherhood. Whereas, few Moms dislike the never-ending laundry the most. They enjoy driving their kids to activities. They hate seeing their child upset which hurt more than anything else.

- Entrepreneur **Chanchal Jain** said, "Finding time for ourselves is a major challenge that most of us face, and it isn't surprising to see many feel torn between meeting their needs and those of their children." In such cases, Moms need to recognise that nurturing their own well-being enhances their ability to be effective caregivers.

- Phonics and spoken English coach **Suman Agarwal** shared, "YOU GROW AS AN INDIVIDUAL. YOU LEARN A LOT FROM YOUR CHILDREN."

- Homemaker **Hema Sharma** accepted, "The best part of motherhood is experiencing every emotion & the worst part is overthinking about their needs and requirements."

- Maharashtra based Educator **Sana Inamdar** said, "The most memorable moments I have experienced are his first words, pretend play, his first walk, first day of school."

- Delhi-based Banker Mom **Poorva Chaturvedi** shared, "It's beautiful journey and gives me purpose and life, but it's also draining and has the capacity to crush my soul at any given moment."

- Alwar-based Homemaker who belongs to Gen X shared, "As my children have grown up, I can share many things with them. I am learning their perspectives and they need me for their moral support. On this stage of my life it's a two-way process now."

- One of the experts from US shared, "Mommy fatigue is a form of exhaustion that occurs as a result of feeling physically and emotionally overwhelmed by mothering."

- Gurugram based HR **Neha Vashistha**, further explained the fact, "An exhausted mom often experiences fears related to not being good enough, relinquishing control, and losing her sense of self." In such case focusing on quality time instead of quantity, would be better solution.

- Homemaker **Lippi Gulati** shared, "For me motherhood is a blessing, I got so many rewards as a mom, when first time they said my name 'mummy,' the first day of their school and when they came back with a big hug, their all prayers belongs to me and yes their first step. Would love to tell you that we do it as a ritual. When our kids take their first step, we make Mithi (sweet)

Roti and roll it to the path they are taking their first steps, and then we eat it as a Prasad. For me it's a blessing when society knows you by the name of your child. I enjoyed and cherish every moment we spent together."

- Jodhpur based Doctor **Nidhi Jain** shared, You become a multitasker, The best part is that kids are your biggest motivation. When you become a mom, you become super-active, and you learn the art of multitasking and start working harder than earlier.

- Alwar based mom **Priya Khandelwal** explained, after you get the tag "Mom" you become stronger, I don't know from where does I got so much of strength after becoming a mom that nothing seem to be difficult as when face of lot challenges then those challenges make you a strong person.

- A homemaker shared, "Over the years, I have learned that it is a great responsibility to rear a life. But I have learned that every child has his own special traits. We don't own them. We feel more complete when we see our children progressing. However, I am a homemaker, so I don't have to balance between children and my career. In the beginning, I didn't think of my personal interests. However, I had more time for my personal interests. My children have always helped me find my own interests. I could find my personal interest in book reading and doodling just because of my daughter."

- **Dr. Shelly Narula Gupta** shared, "When you grow up as Mom with your kids at one point, your role reverse." She further explained, "Me and my teenager and young adult boys try to talk daily and the role has been reversed. Now they are my problem solvers. They teach me the new technology and always ready to help, which is way more satisfying."

7| Mom's Tension

hy Mothers are always worried about certain hazards to their kids? why they are always in tension? why they keeps calling their kids even when they are grown up?

According to our research, Moms are always intense because they themselves are struggling with anxiety or depression (more than 40 % of Moms accepted this fact)

- Another reason is they think, without them, their kids will be bullied by their classmates or other kids. Getting in trouble with the police is another fear of 40 % of Moms.

- During our research, we found a very weird reason: 35% of Moms think that their kids will be kidnapped and they keep telling their kids not to trust anyone because they may be kidnappers.

- Moms are also worried that their kids will get beaten up or attacked by known or unknowns. They are also worried their kids shouldn't be addicted to drugs or alcohol. 10 % of Moms are worried about getting shot.

- One of the major insecurities among teenage kids is getting pregnant or getting someone pregnant. They keep spying on their kids for the same.

- Mobile addiction or porn addiction is also a major threat among teenager's Moms.

- Phonics and spoken English coach Suman Agarwal shared, "CURRENTLY THE AGE THAT MY SONS ARE IN, I HAVE CONCERNS WITH RESPECT TO THEIR INDULGING IN CERTAIN UNDESIRABLE ACTIVITIES."

- Homemaker Mom Hema Sharma shared her worries, "Sometimes I feel parenting is the hardest job in the world, and the biggest tension is to give them a protective atmosphere."

- **Influenced by bad company / friends** – Maharashtra based Educator Sana Inamdar accepted, "Yes I do take stress, I want to bring him as a good and successful human being but what if he comes under bad friends that would be my worst nightmare."

- **Child Safety in the cyber world** - Software Engineer Mom Prachi shared her experience, "In the era of the digital world, ensuring your child's safety is the biggest challenge which I am facing as the kids are prone to xyz content, which is not appropriate as per their age. I have done many things to avoid it and stop it, but after several trials, we were unsuccessful. My whole family tried not giving him and tried to stop his TV, but we couldn't as he started finding other ways to watch because kids are too smart these days. I did a lot of counselling and took the help of school teachers as well to show him the right path, but he didn't agree and was again watching the content, which was not good for growth and brain development."

(The solution she implemented is written in the solution chapter)

8 | Are There Bad Mothers?

This is how society see motherhood. A mother who sacrifices her priorities for her kids is considered a good mother, and the one who does not is considered bad.

Most of the moms & children agreed that there isn't any bad mom exist. This is only the society who label them as good or bad.

9 | Problems Faced by Asian Moms

Asian Moms frequently grapple with the demands of managing both household responsibilities and professional careers. Despite the increasing participation of women in the workforce, they often face challenges such as limited access to affordable childcare, lack of flexible work arrangements, and gender discrimination in the workplace. Marital and family dynamics also play a significant role in shaping the experiences of Indian Moms. In many households, women are expected to uphold familial harmony, often at the expense of their own autonomy and well-being.

While researching this topic, I don't know why not even a single mom agreed to take her name; maybe this is because of societal norms or taboos. But during this specific topic, I myself cried a lot; although we are sitting in the year 2024 when technology is developed, AI is developed, and financial condition is developed at some points, the mentality of society is still struggling and juggling between what to accept and what not.

Anyway, here is my research. Our research is based on the following percentage. We may divide the whole scenario into 3 major parts, also let's find out the answer: Is her life too hard?

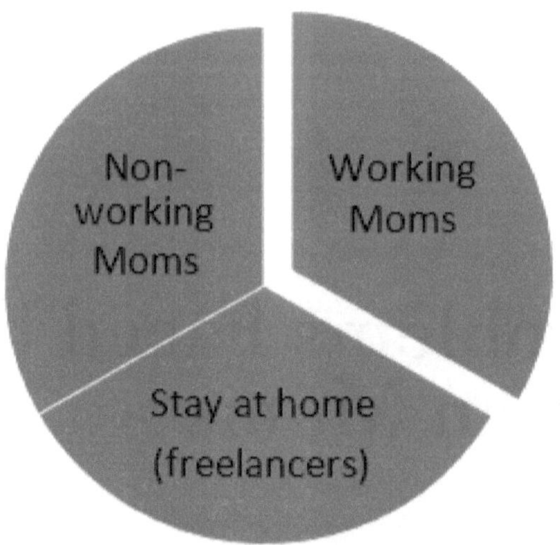

1. Working Mom:

Working Moms face incredible pressure to juggle work and family responsibilities. Indian parents-in-law aren't known to be particularly supportive. So, a typical Indian woman's day begins two hours before everyone else, cooking, packing lunch, making breakfast, and sending kids off to school and only then does she get a chance to get ready for her own day at work. These are the challenges and struggles she faces every day:

Prof. Jyoti Rana, who herself is a renowned author and Registrar at Shri Vishwakarma Skill University, Gurugram enlightened the topic gracefully, She says, "As a working mother, my journey has been a rollercoaster ride of challenges, triumphs, and invaluable lessons. Balancing the demands of a career with the responsibilities of motherhood has tested my resilience, pushed me to my limits, and ultimately shaped me into the woman I am today."

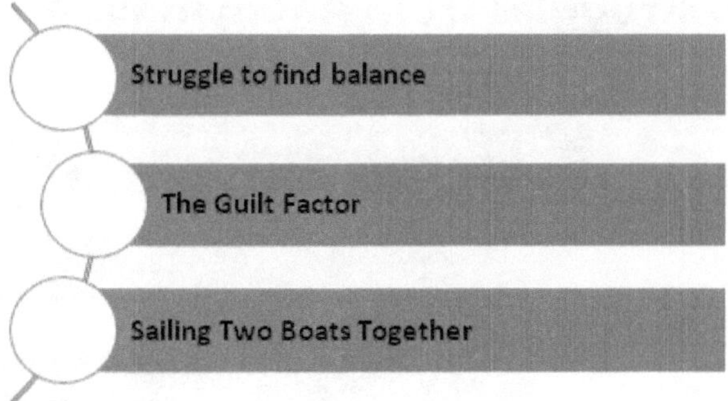

- **Struggle to find balance** - Further, she elaborated, "The challenges I've faced as a mother of a boy and a girl are as diverse as they are daunting. One of the most significant hurdles I encountered was the constant struggle to find balance. Juggling the demands of a full-time job with the needs of my children often felt like walking a tightrope, with each step requiring careful consideration and precision. From early morning meetings to late-night deadlines, finding time to nurture my children's emotional and physical well-being amidst the chaos of work commitments proved to be an ongoing challenge."

- **The Guilt Factor** - She admitted that the guilt of not being able to spend as much time with my children as I would have liked weighed heavily on my heart. Missing school events, bedtime stories, and precious moments with my little ones due to work obligations left me feeling torn and guilty.

- **Sailing Two Boats Together** - She said, "From coordinating schedules to arranging pickups and drop-offs, the logistical hurdles of managing a household while pursuing a career were often overwhelming. Striking a balance between being a devoted mother and pursuing my career ambitions often led to judgement and feelings of inadequacy. The pressure to excel in both realms of life while contending with outdated gender norms and societal expectations often felt like an uphill battle."

Few More struggles from Anonymous Moms

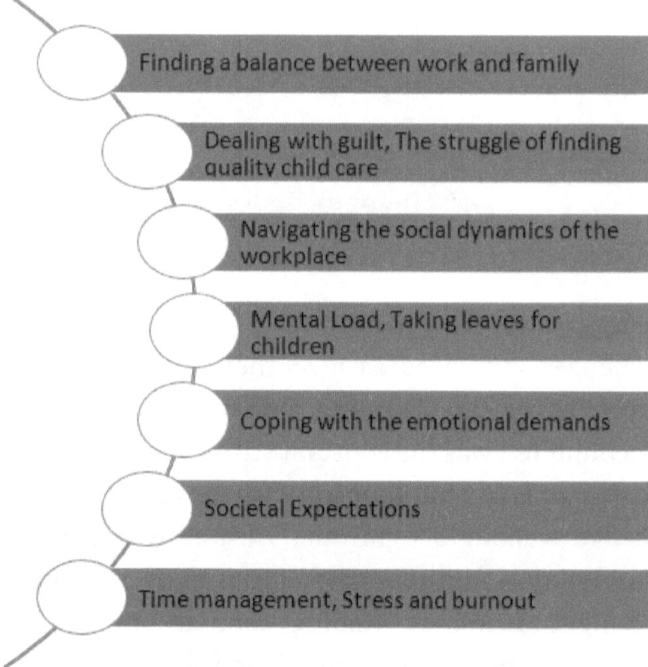

- **Finding a balance between work and family:** Balancing the demands of work and family can be extremely challenging for working Moms. They often have to juggle multiple responsibilities, including childcare, household chores, and professional obligations, leading to feelings of stress and overwhelm.

- **Dealing with guilt:** Many working Moms experience guilt over not spending enough time with their children or not being fully present at work. This guilt can stem from societal expectations and the pressure to excel both professionally and as a parent.

- **The struggle of finding quality child care:** Finding reliable and affordable childcare can be a significant challenge for working Moms. Navigating daycare options, arranging pickups and drop-offs, and managing sick days can add to the already demanding schedule of a working parent.

- **Navigating the social dynamics of the workplace:** Working Moms may face barriers to career advancement, such as limited opportunities for promotion or bias in the workplace. Taking time off for maternity leave or flexible work arrangements can sometimes be perceived negatively by employers, impacting career progression.

- **Mental Load:** Working Moms often carry a disproportionate mental load, including planning and organizing family schedules, coordinating household tasks, and managing childcare arrangements. This mental burden can contribute to feelings of exhaustion and burnout.

- **Taking leaves for children:** It's difficult for a working Mom to take leaves for unofficial events like birthday parties, picnic, PTM, social get together etc. Some on the other day she has to sacrifice by choosing one over others.

- **Coping with the emotional demands:** At growing stage child always need a soft corner to rely on & who is better than a Mom. But as working Mom, she is not available all the time and child has to wait to vent out, slowly-slowly he/ she become unattached with Moms in terms of emotional support.

- **Societal Expectations:** Working Moms may face societal judgement and criticism for prioritizing their careers over full-time caregiving. There can be pressure to conform to traditional gender roles and expectations, leading to feelings of inadequacy or guilt.

- **Time management:** One of the biggest challenges for working mothers is managing their time effectively. Juggling work responsibilities with caring for children can be incredibly difficult, particularly if the mother does not have access to flexible work arrangements or sufficient support at home.

- **Stress and Burnout:** Trying to excel in both their professional and personal lives can lead to high levels of stress and burnout for working Moms. The constant juggling of responsibilities without adequate support can take a toll on their mental and physical well-being.

According to my opinion, these challenges require systemic changes, including policies that support working parents, such as paid parental leave, flexible work arrangements, and affordable childcare options. Additionally, fostering a culture of support and understanding in the workplace can help alleviate some of the pressures faced by working Moms. It's essential to recognise and value the contributions of working Moms while also providing them with the resources and support they need to thrive both at work and at home.

Stay-at-home Mom

Stay-at-home Moms encounter a unique set of challenges that can impact their well-being and sense of fulfilment:

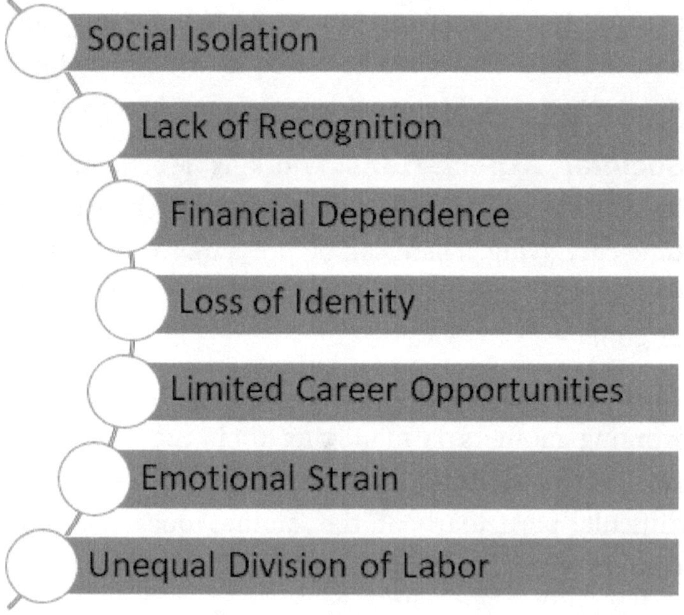

- **Social Isolation**: Being at home full-time can lead to feelings of loneliness and isolation, especially if the mom's social circle consists mainly of working individuals. Limited adult interaction can take a toll on mental health.

- **Lack of Recognition:** Stay-at-home Moms often don't receive the same recognition or validation as those in the workforce. Their contributions to the household and family may go unnoticed, leading to feelings of undervaluation.

- **Financial Dependence:** Relinquishing a career to stay-at-home can lead to financial dependence on a partner. This dependency can create feelings of vulnerability and hinder the mom's ability to make independent financial decisions.

- **Loss of Identity:** Prioritizing caregiving responsibilities over personal pursuits can result in a loss of identity outside of the role of a parent and spouse. Stay-at-home Moms may struggle to maintain a sense of self and personal fulfilment.

- **Limited career Opportunities:** Taking time away from the workforce can impact a stay-at-home mom's career trajectory, making it challenging to re-enter or advance in the workforce later on. This can lead to feelings of career stagnation and loss of professional identity.

- **Emotional Strain:** Balancing the demands of caregiving, household chores, and personal needs can be emotionally draining. Stay-at-home Moms may experience burnout and stress from the constant juggling of responsibilities.

- **Unequal Division of Labour:** In some households, the expectation that the stay-at-home mom will handle all domestic duties can create an unequal division of labour, leading to feelings of resentment and frustration.

- According to me, these challenges requires support systems, including opportunities for social interaction, acknowledgement of the value of caregiving, and access to resources for personal and professional development. It's essential to recognise and validate the contributions of stay-at-home Moms while also addressing the systemic factors that contribute to their challenges.

Single Moms

Single Moms face a multitude of challenges, often having to navigate parenthood alone while balancing work, finances, and personal well-being. One of my friends, who has been facing this problem & going through the process of divorce for the last seven years, elaborated on this topic for me. She doesn't want her name to be published, but she has unfolded many layers of this point.

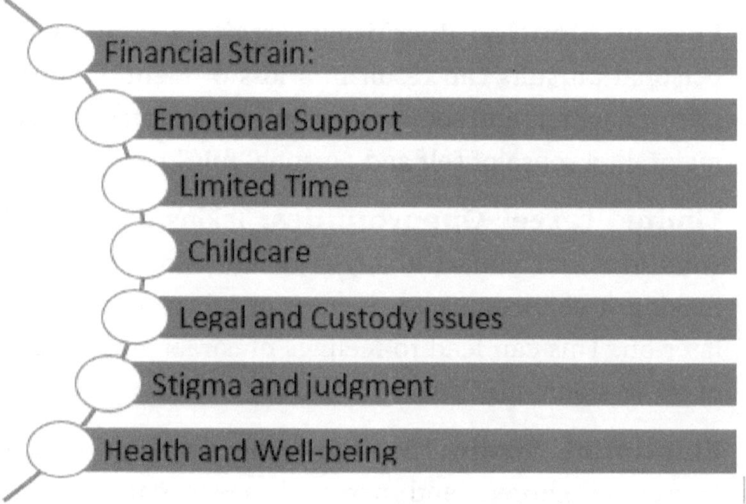

- **Financial Strain:** Single Moms often bear the sole financial responsibility for their families, which can lead to financial instability. Balancing the costs of childcare, housing, education, and healthcare on a single income can be overwhelming.

- **Emotional Support:** Without a partner, single Moms may lack emotional support and face feelings of loneliness and isolation. They may also have to deal with the emotional impact of separation or divorce while trying to support their children through the process.

- **Limited Time:** Single Moms often have to juggle multiple roles, including caregiving, breadwinning, and managing household responsibilities. This can leave little time for self-care or pursuing personal interests and can lead to feelings of exhaustion and burnout.

- **Childcare:** Finding affordable and reliable childcare as a single-parent can be challenging. Single Moms may struggle to balance work schedules with childcare needs and may not have a support system to rely on for backup care.

- **Legal and Custody Issues:** While explaining this point, she cried a lot; she elaborated that it was very difficult for her to take custody of her son coz her ex-husband is having political relations, but for now, because the child is too young to decide, according to court he requires Mom the most, I hope in future she'll get full custody of her only child.

- **Stigma and Judgement:** Single Moms often face stigma and judgement from society, including stereotypes about their abilities to parent effectively or assumptions about their relationship status. This can impact their self-esteem and sense of belonging in their communities.

- **Health and Well-being:** Balancing the demands of single parenthood can take a toll on single Moms' physical and mental health. They may struggle to find time for exercise, proper nutrition, and healthcare appointments, leading to increased stress and risk of health issues.

While listening to her insight story, I highly recommend that single Moms require a multifaceted approach that addresses their financial, emotional, and logistical needs. Providing access to affordable childcare, financial assistance programmes, mental health services, and community support networks can help alleviate some of the challenges faced by single Moms and empower them to thrive as parents and individuals. It's also important to challenge societal stereotypes and stigma surrounding single parenthood and to recognise the resilience and strength of single Moms in raising their children.

Less-educated Moms

It's a saying, "Education is the key to success" When a female is educated, her whole family is educated. Education is not only about degrees and books. It's about self-awareness & accepting new changes and challenges to remain an active member of society. As an uneducated person, they face a variety of challenges that can impact their ability to care for themselves and their families.

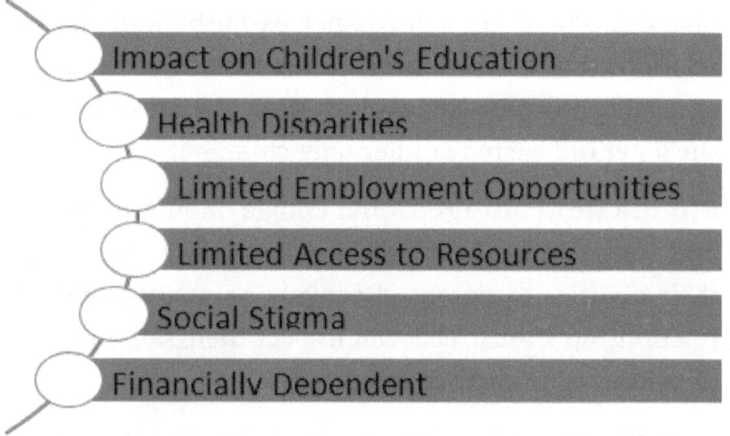

- **Impact on Children's Education:** Undereducated Moms may struggle to support their children's education due to a lack of knowledge or resources. This can impact children's academic performance and future opportunities.

- **Health Disparities:** Less-educated Moms may face health disparities due to a lack of knowledge about healthy behaviors and limited access to healthcare services. This can impact their overall health and well-being.

- **Limited Employment Opportunities:** Without a formal education, these Moms may have difficulty finding stable employment or advancing in their careers. This can lead to financial insecurity and difficulty providing for their families.

- **Limited Access to Resources:** These Moms may struggle to access important resources such as healthcare, childcare, and social services due to a lack of knowledge or resources. This can impact their ability to meet their families' basic needs.

- **Social Stigma:** These Moms may face social stigma and discrimination due to their lack of education. This can impact their self-esteem and sense of belonging in their communities.

- **Financially Dependent:** These Moms have to stay dependent on others for their financial needs. Although few undereducated Moms are well equipped with money and materialistic things, because of their family status, the money they use is given to them by others. Education gives us a feeling of independence and self-worth, which can't be compared with any other thing in this world.

I personally think education in the right way leads to empowerment both in personal & social terms. I would like to request every parent to empower their kids, whether daughter or son, with education because this is the only property that cannot be taken or stolen. Rather than giving dowry, they should be empowered with knowledge and education, and they will thrive in any situation.

Also, the challenges faced by less-educated Moms require a multifaceted approach that includes increasing access to education and vocational training, providing support services and resources, and addressing systemic barriers to education and employment. By empowering less-educated Moms to improve their education and skills, we can help them and their families a better support system and break the cycle of poverty and inequality.

Mom with Special Child

Raising a child with special needs can present unique challenges for mothers. Although, while researching this topic, I found a few Moms who are amazingly positive. Delhi-based teacher and social worker **Seema Arora** is the best example of this. The way she elaborated on the whole process is heart-wrenching. To support her son in education, she did her B Ed. In special education, She said, "I taught him piano, tabla". I personally experienced the way she treats her son Saksham is fabulous.

Further, she said, "Whether you have a normal child or a child with special need, they should be taken care with calmness, politeness, understand their need first, discover their interest and use your mother's magic to draft a full fledge customize programme for your child, if you do so, you and the whole world will see the difference." Really, Hats off to you, Seema Ji.

Society is full of these kinds of examples but we have different people with different mindset. On this topic the scenario is divided in two parts positive and negative, I gave you one example of positive parenting now we have other examples too, here are the challenges these moms face on regular basis.

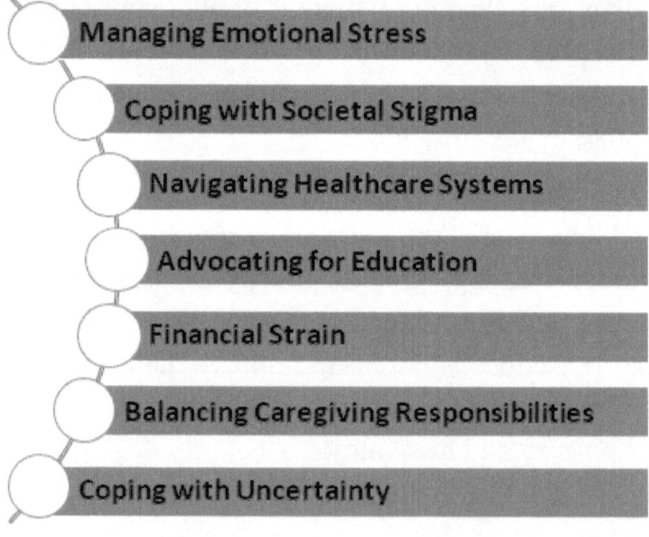

- **Managing Emotional Stress** - Raising a child with special needs can be emotionally challenging for mothers, who may experience feelings of guilt, sadness, frustration, and worry about their child's future. They may also face stress related to managing their own emotions while supporting their child through various challenges.

- **Coping with Societal Stigma** - Moms of children with special needs may encounter societal stigma and negative attitudes from others. This can include judgmental comments, stares, and social isolation, which can be hurtful and demoralizing for both the mother and the child.

- **Navigating Healthcare Systems** - They often have to navigate complex healthcare systems to access appropriate medical care, therapies, and interventions for their child. This can involve coordinating appointments with various specialists, understanding medical terminology, and advocating for their child's needs within the healthcare system.

- **Advocating for Education** - They may need to advocate for their child's educational rights and access to support services such as special education programmes, therapy services, and assistive technologies. This can involve attending Individualized Education Programme (IEP) meetings, communicating with school administrators and teachers, and ensuring that their child's needs are being met in the educational setting.

- **Financial Strain** - Raising a child with special needs often comes with significant financial costs, including medical expenses, therapy services, specialized equipment, and modifications to the home environment. They may face financial strain and worry about how to afford the necessary support for their children. Limited availability of specialized healthcare providers, long waitlists for services, and lack of funding for support programmes.

- **Balancing Caregiving Responsibilities** - Balancing caregiving responsibilities for a child with special needs with other obligations such as work, household tasks, and caring for other family members can be overwhelming for mothers. They may struggle to find time for self-care and may experience burnout from the constant demands of caregiving.

- **Coping with Uncertainty** - They may struggle with feelings of uncertainty about their child's future and the long-term impact of their child's special needs on their family dynamics and relationships. They may grapple with questions about independence, employment opportunities, and social inclusion for their child as they grow older.

I believe raising a child with special needs requires resilience, patience, and a strong support network to help mothers navigate the challenges they may encounter along the way.

"Cheers to the Moms who are doing this job unconditionally"

The so-called Super Mom

Sounds weird, but it's true, we invite a lot of problems with this habit. Remember and note down, "Nothing is perfect in this whole universe, so why we should be" While being a "super mom" may seem admirable, it often comes with its own set of challenges; here are a few mentioned below:

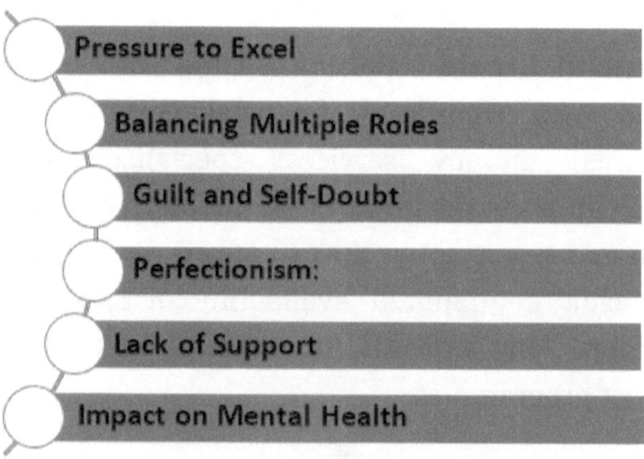

Pressure to Excel: Supermoms often feel immense pressure to excel in every aspect of their lives, including parenting, career, relationships, and personal goals. This pressure can lead to feelings of inadequacy or burnout as they strive to meet unrealistic expectations.

- **Balancing Multiple Roles**: Juggling multiple roles as a caregiver, breadwinner, partner, and individual can be overwhelming for super Moms. They may struggle to find time for self-care and personal interests amidst their many responsibilities.

- **Guilt and Self-Doubt:** Despite their efforts, Super Moms may experience feelings of guilt or self-doubt about their ability to meet all the demands placed upon them. They may worry that they're not doing enough for their families or that they're neglecting their own needs in the process.

- **Perfectionism:** Supermoms may feel compelled to strive for perfection in everything they do, leading to high levels of stress and anxiety. The fear of failure or criticism can drive them to overextend themselves and priorities external validation over their own well-being with unrealistic expectations for their children, perpetuating the cycle of perfectionism and pressure to excel. It's important for super Moms to role model healthy behaviors and priorities balance and self-care to set a positive example for their families.

- **Lack of Support:** Supermoms may feel like they have to do it all on their own, without adequate support from partners, family members, or communities. This lack of support can exacerbate feelings of isolation and overwhelm.

- **Impact on mental health**: The constant pressure to be a "super mom" can take a toll on mental health, leading to symptoms of anxiety, depression, or burnout. It's essential for super Moms to priorities self-care and seek support when needed to maintain their well-being.

I am working on the mental health Awareness Programme under Mission Purple. I found that nowadays, Moms are putting too much pressure on them to prove themselves best, but this habit of becoming so-called Super Mom is moving them to the road of anxiety and depression. So, Moms, be relaxed and don't take too much pressure; everything will be okay.

10| Mom Syndrome

After talking about the challenges, we mom face every day, Let's talk about a few Mom Syndromes.

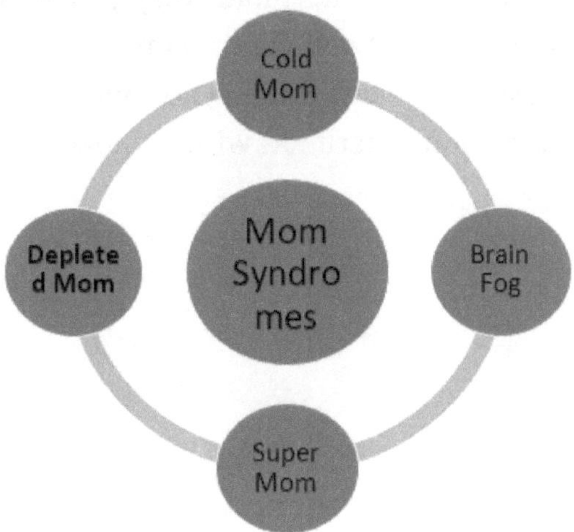

1. **Cold Mom Syndrome** - is where one's maternal figure is emotionally absent. Emotionally cold mothers put a psychological distance between themselves and their children. Cold mothers may not appear happy, fulfilled, or excited by their children's growth and accomplishments.

2. **Mom Brain Fog** - small studies support the existence of a cognitive change after birth, causing forgetfulness, fogginess and a feeling of being scatterbrained.

3. **Super Mom Syndrome** – or sacrificing supermom syndrome, the delusional belief of a mother genetically hardwired to priorities all things for all people in her life while sublimating her own needs. It is romanticized by cinema and propagated by social media.

4. **Depleted Mom** – It refers to a state of physical, mental, and emotional exhaustion experienced by mothers, often resulting from the demands of childcare, household responsibilities, and possibly work or other commitments. This syndrome can lead to feelings of burnout, stress, and a sense of being overwhelmed.

My Suggestion - It's important for mothers experiencing these kinds of problems to seek support and take steps to priorities self-care. These syndromes don't make you a bad mom, they just indicate that you're stretched thin and in need of self-care. Many women struggle to take time for self-care as Moms, and these syndromes are often a result of the extreme demands of motherhood without adequate support or rest.

11| Today's Moms

As we are standing on the threshold of Generation Alpha and waiting to welcome Generation Beta. If we talk about Moms, right now, there are Moms from three main generations who hold the command of our future adults. These are **Generation X** (mainly playing the role of Grandmothers or elderly Moms of family, with rich experience of raising two generations), **Generation Y**/ Millennials (80% of Moms falls in this category, joining hand in hand, holding four generations together, learning and experiencing new everyday) & **Generation Z** (Early Gen Z/ New Moms, techno-friendly, influencers, social media experts)

Let's explore more about these Moms in detail:

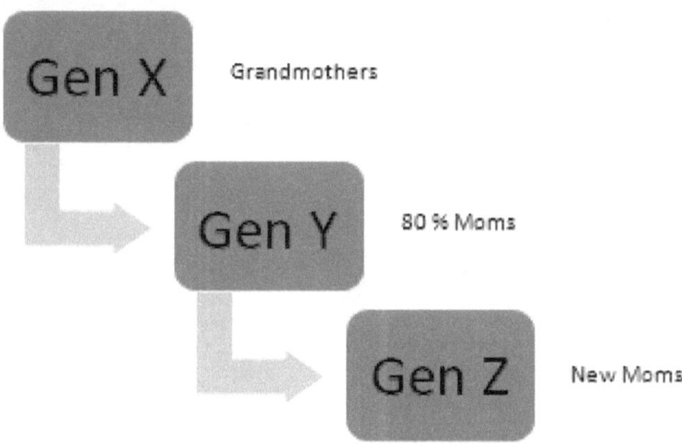

Gen X Moms

In today's era, these are the eldest generation of our society, So let's start our conversation with the most experienced generations, who are playing the role of grandparents these days.

While writing down in the club I came across a group of Moms, who belong to this age group, As I briefed my project to them, they immediately got ready to share their experience on this topic. We had long conversations about many topics.

Mrs Shashi Jain elaborated that now the times has changed, we were only involved in household chores, and we didn't even realize how our kids grew up because, at that time, the scenario was different; the culture of the joint family was followed. So, kids were the grandparents' responsibility instead of the mother and fathers. At that time, fathers were supposed to work outside the home, taking care of the financial needs of the family, and mothers were supposed to maintain household work; because of gender differences, boys were getting priority in everything.

This conversation with these experienced females blew my mind; my perception changed, and my point of view changed. During the research and with my own experience handling this generation, my mom and mother-in-law and a few females I know personally have gone through the trauma of the patriarchy system. Every mom is not the same; you just need to identify and feel their emotions, you'll get the answer as I got.

Challenges faced by Gen X Moms

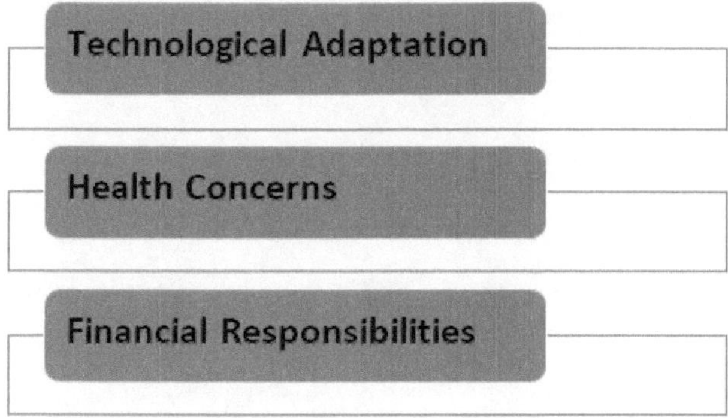

- **Technological Adaptation** - Some Gen X moms may struggle to keep pace with rapidly evolving technology and digital trends, which can impact their ability to stay connected with their children and navigate digital parenting challenges.

- **Health Concerns** - As Gen X moms are ageing, they may face health concerns, such as menopause, vitamin D deficiency, bones problem, knee problem, sugar or BP problem, chronic health conditions, and caregiving responsibilities for their grandchildren, which can impact their overall well-being.

- **Financial Responsibilities** - Gen X moms often bear significant financial responsibilities, such as helping their children in establishing their careers, retirement savings and planning, which can add stress and pressure to their daily lives.

Few Facts about Gen X Moms

(Misconceptions to bust)

1. **They are Rigid** - It's important to note that not all Gen X moms are rigid, and generalizations about any generation should be approached with caution. However, some Gen X moms may exhibit traits that could be perceived as rigidity due to various factors:

Reason of Rigidness	Personal Experiences
	Cultural Influences
	Parenting Trends of the Time
	Desire of stability

- **Personal Experiences** - Our experiences shape our parenting styles and Gen X moms may have experienced challenges or trauma in their own lives that influence their approach to parenting. This could lead to a more structured or rule-based parenting style that might be perceived as rigid by others.

- **Cultural Influences** - Gen X grew up during a period of significant social and economic change, including increased divorce rates and dual-income households. Some Gen X moms may have developed a sense of responsibility and discipline in response to these cultural shifts, which could manifest as rigidity in their parenting style.

- **Parenting Trends of the Time** - Gen X era may have emphasized discipline, structure, and adherence to rules. These moms may have internalized these messages and incorporated them into their parenting style, leading to perceptions of rigidity.

- **Desire for Stability** - Gen X grew up during a time of economic uncertainty and rapid social change. As parents, they may priorities stability and structure in their children's lives as a way to provide a sense of security and predictability.

Conclusion:- It's essential to recognise that rigidity in parenting style can have both positive and negative effects, and individual differences among Gen X moms should be acknowledged. Additionally, societal and cultural factors play a significant role in shaping parenting behaviors across generations.

Are they changing?

As per Mrs. Shashi Jain & her friends, "Like any generation, Gen X moms are evolving and adapting their parenting styles over time. While some may exhibit traits that could be perceived as rigid, many are also embracing more flexible and inclusive approaches to parenting." Here are some points she shared that Gen X moms are changing with time:

How Gen-X Moms are changing	
	Reassessment of Traditional Gender Roles
	Adoption of New Parenting Trends
	Financial Independency
	Embracing Technology
	Emphasis on Emotional Well-being

- **Reassessment of Traditional Gender Roles** – Gen X moms are challenging traditional gender roles and stereotypes, both within their families and in society at large. They are promoting gender equality, shared parenting responsibilities, and respect for diverse identities and experiences.

- **Adoption of New Parenting Trends** - Gen X moms are increasingly incorporating new parenting trends and approaches, such as positive parenting, mindfulness, and child-led learning. They are open to learning from newer generations and adjusting their parenting styles accordingly.

- **Financial Independency** – They are working and also helping their daughters and daughter in laws to thrive, many of us can work, can go out, can do freelancing because of their efforts. Although as any other generation Gen X moms are too divided in two parts but now the ratio of understanding Mother in law is raised by 60%.

- **Embracing Technology** - As technology continues to advance, Gen X moms are becoming more comfortable with digital tools and platforms, which can facilitate communication, access to information, and connection with other parents. They are utilizing online resources, social media, and parenting apps to support their parenting journey.

- **Emphasis on Emotional Well-being** - Gen X moms are placing a greater emphasis on the emotional well-being of their children, recognizing the importance of nurturing their mental health and resilience. They are encouraging open communication, empathy, and self-expression within their families.

- As per the conversation and experience I can conclude that, Gen X moms are adapting to the changing landscape of parenthood, embracing new ideas and approaches while also drawing on their own experiences and values. As they continue to navigate the complexities of modern parenting, they are contributing to a diverse and dynamic parenting culture that reflects the evolving needs and aspirations of families today.

The solution to their problems

Solutions given by experts:	Embrace Flexibility
	Trust Your Instincts
	Practice Self-Care
	Create Boundaries
	Communicate Openly
	Find Your Support System
	Celebrate Imperfection & Enjoy the Journey

- **Embrace Flexibility** - Be open to adjusting your plans and expectations as needed. Flexibility is key to navigating the unpredictable nature of motherhood and life in general. Practice continuous learning and skill development, particularly in areas such as technology and digital literacy, which will help you to stay relevant in today's rapidly changing world.

- **Trust Your Instincts** - You know your child better than anyone else. Trust your instincts and intuition when making parenting decisions, and don't be afraid to advocate for what you believe is best for your child.

- **Practice Self-Care** - Take care of yourself physically, mentally, and emotionally. Self-care isn't selfish—it's essential for maintaining your well-being and being able to care for your family effectively. Priorities Quality Time Focus on creating meaningful moments with your children, whether it's through shared activities, conversations, or simply spending time together. Quality time is often more important than quantity. Implement health and wellness programmes that address the unique health concerns of Gen X moms, such as menopause management, stress reduction techniques, and preventative healthcare measures.

- **Create Boundaries** - Establish clear boundaries and routines to provide structure and stability for your family. Boundaries help maintain balance and harmony in your relationships and daily life.

- **Communicate Openly** - Foster open communication within your family, encouraging honesty, respect, and empathy. Create a safe space where everyone feels comfortable expressing their thoughts, feelings, and concerns.

- **Find Your Support System** - Surround yourself with a supportive network of family, friends, and fellow parents who understand and empathies with your experiences. Lean on them for advice, encouragement, and assistance when needed. Be a positive role model for your children by demonstrating values such as kindness, resilience, responsibility, and integrity in your words and actions.

- **Celebrate Imperfection & Enjoy the Journey** - Embrace the messiness and imperfection of parenting. Nobody has it all figured out, and it's okay to make mistakes along the way. Learn from them, grow, and don't be too hard to yourself. Motherhood is a journey filled with ups and downs, joys and challenges. Embrace the journey, savor the moments, and cherish the memories you create with your love once.

GEN Y MOMS

We are Millennials or Gen Y Moms! We may be "secret introverts." We may be growing up in a world with more advanced technology than previous generations. As a result, we tend to be more comfortable using technology in our daily lives.

As I also belong to this generation, I have my own experience too for add on. Most of the Moms I talked to belong to this generation; almost

65% of this is because of the same mindset, the same problems or the same kind of children we are raising. Anyways back to the topic, most of the Moms in today's world belong to this specific generation, almost 80 % (which is a huge number).

Once Millennials reach motherhood, our research shows, almost 11% are even more interested in crafts & DIY. Social media channels enable these Moms to curate, share and show off their projects; in fact, 38% of Millennial Mothers use Pinterest, and 33% use Instagram.

Gen Y Moms are different

Millennial Moms are also known for being more receptive to new parenting techniques and embracing changing societal norms. They tend to be supportive of a child's interests, fostering creativity, and often involve children in decision-making processes. They're making parenting all their own by sharing responsibilities, breaking gender stereotypes, keeping their passions as a priority, and being "real" with their kids.

They look for ways to be more "present" and involved, and let their kids be part of the decision-making process. Breaking away from "helicopter parenting," they give their kids choices. Open-minded. empathetic. questioning.

They tend to have very positive views of themselves and are very optimistic about their expectations for their lives and they're more likely to say that they're above average compared to their peers and they tend to score higher on other measures of positive self-views.

Dads are Different, Too

From time invested in parenting to valuing closer relationships with their children, millennial fathers are more engaged and involved than ever. Nearly four times as many fathers as in the 1990s now take paternity leave after the birth of a child; according to our research, we have noticed, Dads have evolved in their parenting style over the years, becoming more involved and hands-on in caregiving responsibilities.

Traditionally seen as the breadwinners and disciplinarians, many dads now actively participate in tasks like diaper changing, feeding, and emotional support. This shift reflects broader societal changes towards more equitable parenting roles. **Delhi-based Banker Poorva** said, "My husband not only supports taking care of our little angel but also helps with household chores; I am blessed."

The changes in dad's parenting style include greater involvement in child-rearing tasks like cooking, cleaning, and attending to emotional needs. Many dads are more present in their children's lives, participating in activities, attending school events, and actively engaging in conversations about their interests and feelings. This shift reflects a move towards more collaborative and equal parenting partnerships within families.

Traditional dads typically adhered to traditional gender roles, where they were primarily responsible for providing financial stability for the family and enforcing discipline while leaving most of the caregiving and emotional support to the mother. Modern dads, on the other hand, are more actively involved in all aspects of parenting. They share caregiving responsibilities, participate in household chores, and priorities spending quality time with their children. Modern dads often strive for a more equal partnership with their partners, embracing a more nurturing and hands-on approach to parenting.

Challenges Faced by Dads

New dads face various challenges as they navigate their roles and responsibilities in parenting; some common challenges include:

1. **Social expectations and stereotypes** - New dads may face pressure to conform to traditional gender roles and expectations, which can create internal conflict and external stress.

2. **Balancing work and family life** - Juggling the demands of work while being present and engaged in their children's lives can be challenging for new dads.

3. **Sleep deprivation** - Newborns often disrupt sleep patterns, leading to fatigue and exhaustion for both parents, including dads.

4. **Learning new skills** - Adjusting to tasks like diaper changing, soothing a crying baby, and managing household chores can be overwhelming for new dads who may not have had much experience with childcare before.

5. **Finding support** - New dads may struggle to find support networks and resources tailored to their specific needs and experiences, as much of the focus in parenting support is often directed towards mothers.

6. **Adjusting to changes in the relationship** - Becoming parents can shift the dynamics of a relationship, requiring new dads to navigate changes in communication, intimacy, and division of responsibilities with their partners.

Banker Poorva said, "These challenges requires open communication, flexibility, and a willingness to seek support from partners, family, friends, and community resources, I am blessed in this way."

Tips for Dads

According to our new Moms and a few new dads, here are a few tips you may follow.

1. **Communicate Openly** - Foster strong communication with your children by actively listening to them, validating their feelings, and engaging in meaningful conversations.

2. **Embrace Flexibility** - Be adaptable and willing to adjust your parenting approach as your children grow and their needs change.

3. **Share Responsibilities** - Embrace an equal partnership with your partner in parenting and household tasks. Share caregiving responsibilities, such as feeding, bathing, and bedtime routines.

4. **Be Present** - Make an effort to be actively involved in your children's lives, whether it's attending school events, playing with them, or helping with homework.

5. **Make Time for Bonding** - Set aside dedicated time to bond with your children through activities they enjoy, such as reading together, playing sports, or exploring nature.

6. **Be a Positive Role Model** - Lead by example and demonstrate qualities like respect, empathy, and resilience. Show your children what it means to be a responsible, compassionate, and engaged member of society.

7. **Seek Support** - Build a network of support, including other dads, friends, family members, and parenting groups. Don't hesitate to ask for help or seek professional guidance when needed.

8. **Priorities Self-Care** - Take care of your own physical, mental, and emotional well-being. Get enough rest, exercise regularly, and find healthy ways to manage stress.

9. **Celebrate Milestones** - Cherish and celebrate special moments and achievements with your children, whether big or small. Create lasting memories that you'll both treasure for years to come.

10. **Be Patient and Forgiving** - Parenting is a learning process, and it's okay to make mistakes. Be patient with yourself and your children, and learn from each experience to become a better parent.

What Previous Generation Thinks About Gen Y

When you think of the 'Millennial,' what pops into you head? For many, negative descriptions such as egotistic, demanding and lazy come to mind. However, this is a built-up stereotype that's created undesirable perceptions of the younger generation, especially when concerning the world of work!

Challenges of Gen Y Moms

Gen Y Moms, like any other generation, face a unique set of challenges. They are more likely to experience anxiety, depression, and stress than any previous generation of Moms.

According to our research work, 3 in 4 millennial Moms practice gentle parenting, nearly half (46%) of millennial Moms feel burned out navigating a digital world, 65% believe social media creates unrealistic parenting expectations, and 1 in 4 don't double check parenting advice from social media.

During the research, Moms from different backgrounds shared many challenges they are facing while raising their kids:

Struggles of Gen Y Moms	
	Struggle to Find Balance
	The Guilt Factor
	Sailing Two Boats Together
	Monitoring and Privacy
	Juggling Life
	Dealing with societal expectations
	Maintaining mental and physical well-being
	Feel Unappreciated
	Burdened by the fear of failure
	Rising costs of living and Managing finances

Prof. Jyoti Rana, who herself is a renowned author and Registrar at Shri Vishwakarma Skill University, Gurugram, enlightened the topic gracefully; she shared a few key points:

- **Struggle to find balance** - Further, she elaborated, "The challenges I've faced as a mother of a boy and a girl are as diverse as they are daunting. One of the most significant hurdles I encountered was the constant struggle to find balance."

- **The Guilt Factor** - She admitted that the guilt of not being able to spend as much time with my children as I would have liked weighed heavily on my heart.

- **Sailing the Two Boats Together** - Striking a balance between being a devoted mother and pursuing my career ambitions often led to judgement and feelings of inadequacy.

HR Neha Vashistha, who is working in an MNC in Gurugram, further added the facts:

- **Monitoring and Privacy**- It can be challenging for parents to monitor their children's online activities, especially as children become more independent and start using multiple devices. Many Moms are concerned about their child's privacy online and worry about who has access to their child's personal information.

- **Juggling Life** - Moms who become stay-at-home Moms are juggling their feelings and concerns on top of worrying about their children's emotions.

One of Mom working in private sector shared her feeling as anonymous.

- **Dealing with Societal Expectations** – Society expects us to follow such norms, and if we don't follow them, they boycott the Moms and their parenting style.

- **Maintaining mental and physical well-being -** amid the pressures of modern parenting can add to the complexity of their experiences.

- **Feel Unappreciated** – After doing so much for kids and family, they never get appreciated. Whether they are homemaker Moms, working Moms or freelancer Moms, they give their 200% for a family as compared to any other member, but they are treated for granted by everyone and, their all efforts remain unnoticed.

- **Burdened by the fear of failure** – At every step of parenting, there are so many judgmental people keeping an eye on her; they just wait for one mistake, and all her efforts vanish. She always works under the pressure of failure.

- **Rising costs of living and Managing finances** – Today, the cost of living is very high, school fees, tuition fees, extracurricular activities, and childcare facilities. In fact, birthday parties are so expensive, for a middle-class person, these all are luxury things. So, maintaining standards and giving the life of our kid's choice is high maintenance, which is again a burden on Mom and Dad.

- **Take Advantage from Grandparents** - Software Engineer Prachi said, "At this age, a child can do most of the things by himself, but I had to struggle a lot to make him do things on his own at a very slow pace because every time I ask to do the things he simply goes to his grandmother for the help."

- **Balancing things** with a joint family is never easy. I want to make a comeback in my career after my career break. I had to take a career break of 4 years. I kept on giving interviews and preparing for the job interviews as I had a strong desire and passion to pursue my career.

- **People started judging** I was on a career break, and I couldn't see any ray of hope to restart my career as my mood swings made me burst into anger without any reason, and people around me started judging me for that.

- **24*7 job is more difficult - Software Engineer Prachi** said, "Doing the mommy duty is more difficult than doing a 9-5 job and balancing both the things together takes a lot of effort."

- **YouTube concern -** Sometimes, I am stressed regarding the channels he watches on YouTube, and I ask him to try some good movies. He never watches cartoons which we used to watch as a kid instead, he loves watching random vlogs which are guiding him in the wrong manner, and he adapts it very quickly.

- **Treat all the kids as individuals - Homemaker Lippi Gulati** said, "It felt like a challenge in the initial setting, but gradually it came to me as a learning. My firstborn was a peaceful toddler, and after five years, when my second was born, she was the complete opposite. She was a moody toddler. Initially, it was quite difficult to understand her, but I learned a lesson that every child is different in his/her own way. We should always treat them as an individual."

- **Evolving journey** Lippi Gulati said, "In my way, evolution is the part of motherhood because every day you learn something new about the behavior of your child. We can teach things to our children, but I think the motherhood is the only way by which every woman learn from her kids. And the experience of her is different for her each and every child."

- **Sole Provider of Emotional Support –** Educator Sana Inamdar said, "Sometimes it is difficult to handle the pressure of being the sole provider of emotional support for my child, but now he is growing he is becoming practical to it."

- **They are Pro and Never Take Anything Lesser Than That -** Educator Suman Agarwal said, "THEY WILL ALWAYS TRY TO SHOW AND PROVE THAT THEY ARE A 'PRO.' AND I WON'T BE WILLING TO TAKE ANYTHING LESSER THAN THAT FROM YOU!"

- **Work & Personal life balance** - Dr. Shelly Narula, who is a Dentist by degree and a jwellery Designer by heart and profession, shared that it's really difficult to manage both together, and now it's your smartness how you'll manage both together. But in this battle, I always priorities my family over work.

- **Children's Connection to Culture While Staying in Abroad -** Gurmeet Bindra, who is a full-time working mom in the healthcare, field shared, "As an immigrant mother in Canada I had apprehension and additional responsibility to ensure my children are connected to their culture. Later on, I resolve this challenge with the help of few constant decisions."

Weakness of Gen Y Moms

Every challenge that we face is because of our few weaknesses. During the research, a few of the experts mentioned that because of certain weaknesses, we, as Moms, have to face many challenges or problems. According to them if we focus on overcoming these weaknesses, we may overcome our challenges.

Weakness of Gen Y Moms	
	Devalue Face-to-Face Communication
	Dependent on Feedback
	Fixated on Flexibility
	Poor Work Ethic
	Career Impatience
	Frequently Job Hop
	Lack of Experience

Devalue Face-to-Face Communication – Educator Surbhi said, "We Moms are so busy with our kids & family that we don't have time to communicate with our extended family or friends." In fact, during the research, most of the Moms accepted that they devalue face-to-face communication or that they don't have time to do it. It can have negative consequences. It may contribute to feelings of isolation, social disconnection, and misunderstanding. Additionally, relying too heavily on digital communication can hinder the development of essential interpersonal skills, such as active listening and conflict resolution, which are cultivated through real-life interactions. Priorities it in our personal and professional lives. Whether it's scheduling regular meetups with friends and family or promoting face-to-face interactions in the workplace, fostering meaningful connections in person is essential for building strong, resilient communities.

- **Dependent on Feedback** – Centre head Sushma accepted, "Feedback can play a valuable role in helping Moms gauge their effectiveness as parents, validate their choices, and identify areas for improvement." She further elaborated, "Constructive feedback increases your value, but Moms who constantly seek validation from others may experience heightened anxiety, self-doubt, or feelings of inadequacy if the feedback they receive is negative or conflicting." She said, "I have seen few Moms actively seek feedback from others, whether it's from family members, friends, or professionals whereas others may be more self-assured in their parenting decisions and rely less on external input." It's essential for Moms to strike a balance between seeking feedback and trusting their own instincts and judgement as parents.

- **Fixated on Flexibility** – One of the leading yoga experts explained, "Fixation refers to a rigid adherence to certain ideas, beliefs, or behaviors, often to the point of stubbornness or resistance to change." On the other hand, "flexibility involves the willingness and ability to adapt to changing circumstances, embrace new ideas, and adjust one's behavior accordingly."

She further advised, "Finding the right balance between fixated behaviors and flexibility is essential for optimal functioning and well-being. Too much fixation can lead to stagnation, rigidity, and missed opportunities for growth, while excessive flexibility may result in lack of direction and inconsistency."

- **Poor Work Ethic** – This may sound weird, but many of the working Moms accept the fact that they are blamed at workplaces for poor work ethics. But I believe, it all depends upon individual values, personal circumstances, and societal pressures. Instead of focusing on perceived weaknesses, it's more constructive to support all individuals, including Moms, in achieving a healthy work-life balance and fulfilling their professional and personal goals.

- **Career Impatience** – Again, it depends upon the circumstances of the individual. A mom working in a private limited company shared with us that because of her first child, she couldn't spend much time and energy at the office, so she was called "career impatience" & she doesn't have a work ethic. As every coin has two sides, sometimes because of circumstances & sometimes because of a lack of willingness to invest the time and effort, this impetuousness occurs. For long-term growth, you need to be consistent. Career impatience may miss out on valuable learning experiences, opportunities for skill development, and the cultivation of meaningful relationships in the workplace. Moreover, constantly chasing short term gains can lead to burnout, dissatisfaction, and a lack of fulfilment in the long run.

- **Frequently Job Hop** – HR Neha revealed, "Another major factor or weakness of working mom is job hop, again it's not because of willingness, sometimes or many times in mom's life it's a major issue. Wedding leave, maternity leave, leave for taking care of child leads to job hop." Employers may view job hoppers as unreliable or lacking commitment, which can make it challenging to secure employment with reputable companies or advance in one's career. One's professional trajectory makes it difficult to build expertise in a particular field or establish long-term relationships with colleagues and mentors.

- **Lack of Experience** – A famous gynecologist said, "Motherhood brings lots of new experiences for any female, mostly 1st-time mommies face this kind of issue; just like any other jobs, it needs learning by doing the process. Lacking experience is the feeling of insecurity and self-doubt. New Moms may struggle to assess their abilities accurately or feel ill-equipped to handle new challenges. This can lead to anxiety, fear of failure, and reluctance to take risks. By acknowledging limitations and seeking support and guidance, they may learn and explore the new phase of motherhood and embrace its beauty without compromising their physical and mental health."

Generation Z Moms

Gen Z Moms, born after 1996, bring a unique perspective to motherhood shaped by their upbringing in a digitally connected world. Although I belongs to Gen Y but I personally like the style and approach of this new generation, in fact few of them are really good friend of mine. While talking to them I learned a lot and trying to implement on my kids who belongs to Gen Alpha.

Characteristics of Gen Z Moms	**Tech-Savvy Moms**
	Entrepreneur
	Budget - Friendly Parenting
	Balancing between Digital and Real Life
	Online Communities and Support Networks
	Embracing Progressive Parenting Styles
	Awareness About Mental Health
	Embrace Diversity and Inclusivity
	Environment friendly and sustainability
	Prioritizing their Careers Above anything
	Love for Gaming on Smartphones
	Less Opportunities to Develop Social Skills

Let's find out their unique specialty based on research with these new Moms:

* **The Tech-Savvy Moms** - Generation Z Moms are adept at using technology to manage their roles as mothers. They rely heavily on parenting apps, social media groups, and online resources for advice, support, and networking with other Moms.

- **Entrepreneur** - Most of these Moms are, leveraging their digital skills to work from home or start their own businesses while juggling the demands of motherhood. They value flexibility and autonomy in their careers.

- **Budget-Friendly** Parenting - One of the coolest things I found while talking to them is budget-friendly parenting. Despite their tech-savviness and entrepreneurial spirit, Generation Z Moms may face financial challenges, such as student loan debt and high living costs. They priorities financial stability and may seek out budget-friendly parenting solutions.

- **Balancing between Digital and Real-Life** – Gen Z moms understand the importance of limiting screen time for their children while also leveraging technology for educational purposes and entertainment. They strive to find a balance between the digital world and real-life experiences. With the prevalence of social media, Generation Z Moms navigate the challenges of parenting in the public eye. They carefully curate their online presence, balancing authenticity with privacy concerns for themselves and their children.

- **Online Communities and Support Networks** - Gen Z moms rely on connecting with other parents facing similar challenges. They seek validation, advice, and solidarity in these virtual spaces.

- **Embracing Progressive Parenting Styles** – Gen Z Moms focus on open communication, empathy, and individuality. They are more likely to challenge traditional gender roles and parenting norms.

- **Awareness About mental health** - Generation Z Moms priorities their own well-being as well as that of their children. They are more open to discussing mental health issues and seeking professional help when needed.

- **Embracing Diversity and Inclusivity** – Gen Z moms celebrating cultural differences and teaching their children to respect and appreciate diversity in all its forms.

- **Environment-friendly and sustainability** – These things influence the parenting choices of Generation Z Moms. They are more likely to choose eco-friendly products, promote recycling, and educate their children about environmental issues.

- **Prioritizing their Careers Above Anything** – Gen Z moms' priorities their careers and wellness above settling down and starting a family. While doing deep research and talking to a few Moms personally, I noticed that many Gen Z moms may not want to follow the paths of previous generations.

- **Gaming On Smartphones** - If there's one thing this generation loves to do, is games. It's a hugely popular pastime for this group, particularly when gaming on smartphones. Almost 9 in 10 Gen Z games on any device. What sets Gen Z apart from other generations is their love for gaming.

- **Less Opportunities to Develop Social Skills** - One more thing I realized over a period, that growing up with smartphones and social media during formative childhood and adolescence years could lead to increased shyness as Generation Z may have had fewer opportunities to develop social skills and which may lead to greater social anxiety and shyness.

In conclusion, I can say, "Generation Z Moms bring a blend of digital fluency, progressive values, and entrepreneurial spirit to the journey of motherhood, shaping the landscape of parenting in the 21st century. Although right now there are only 20% of Moms are from Gen Z, but slowly-slowly this percentage is growing."

12 | The Hardest Age of Parenting

As per our research, every mom said that the age they are handling right now is the most difficult age. According to the ratio, from toddler tantrums to teen attitude, parenting children at any age can be tough. Some people find it hard to parent children in their middle school years. Puberty and peer pressure can leave these teens feeling angry, alone, and confused, which can cause bad behavior and disagreements.

According to my deep research and personal experience, Keep aside the terrible twos and the hateful teens, the most challenging stage for parents is when their child is going through puberty, and their independence is still shaky and unbalanced. As per the personal conversation with Moms in my family and a few close friends, here are the numerous challenges Moms face during their child's puberty:

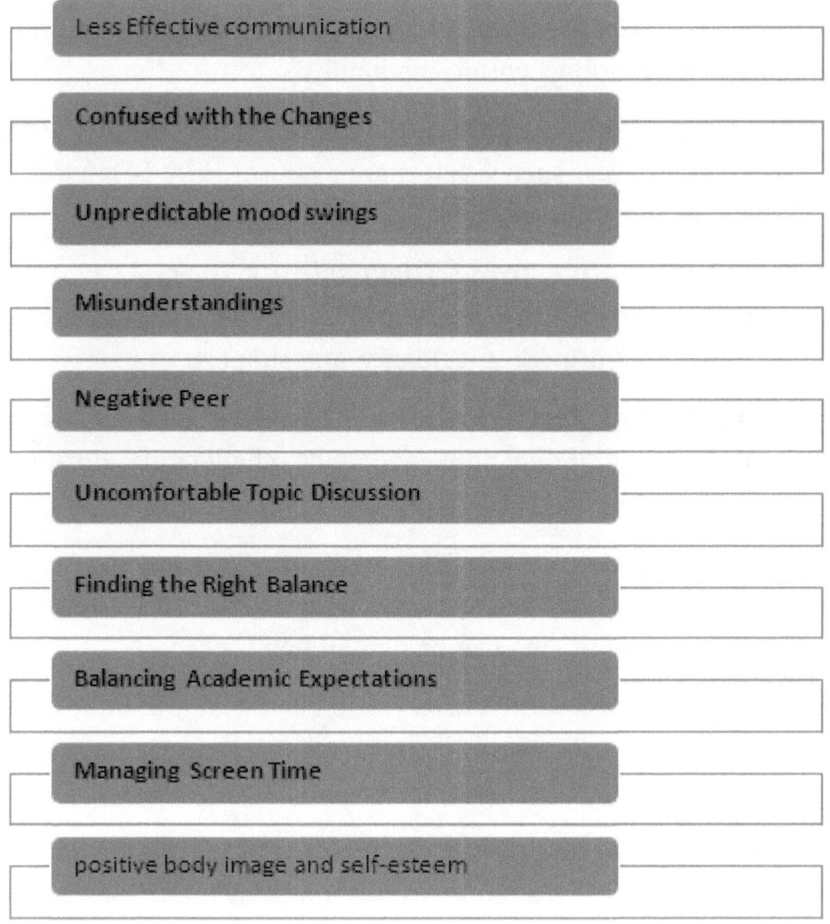

- **Less Effective Communication** - It becomes more challenging as adolescents may withdraw or become less open about their experiences.

- **Confused with the Changes** - Moms need to navigate their child's physical, emotional, and psychological changes, which can be confusing and overwhelming for both.

- **Unpredictable mood swings** and emotional outbursts can strain the mom-child relationship.

- **Misunderstandings** - Adolescents may question their identity and experiment with different persons, leading to conflicts and misunderstandings within the family.

- **Negative Peer** - Moms must help their children resist negative peer influences, such as substance abuse, risky behaviors, and social media pressure.

- **Uncomfortable Topic Discussion** - Topics like sexuality, consent, and healthy relationships can be uncomfortable but necessary for providing guidance and support.

- **Finding the Right Balance** - between being authoritative and allowing independence can be challenging during this transitional period.

- **Balancing Academic Expectations** - Balancing Academic Expectations and performance while supporting their child's emotional well-being can be demanding for Moms.

- **Managing Screen Time** – For all the Moms online safety, and social media influence becomes increasingly important as adolescents spend more time online.

- **Positive Body Image and Self-Esteem** - Helping their child develop amidst societal pressures and media representations of beauty can be difficult.

13 | The Big Question

Are Parents Responsible for Developing a Child's Habits?

Parents play a significant role in shaping a child's habits, as they serve as primary influencers during their formative years.

According to the principal of a famous school in NCR explained, "Parents are a big role model to their children, who want to be just like them. The poor habits of parents (i.e., drugs, smoking), rubs off onto children and they are often too young to know what is right and wrong."

Further, she elaborated that parents are not solely responsible for all aspects of a child's habits; their actions, guidance, and environment greatly impact a child's development.

Through modelling healthy behaviors, providing structure, and offering guidance, parents can positively influence habits related to nutrition, exercise, hygiene, social interactions, and more.

However, external factors such as peers, media, and societal influences also contribute to a child's habits as they grow older.

Therefore, while parents are influential, they share responsibility with other factors in shaping a child's habits.

14 | Do Moms Control Their Kids?

One funny fact about this question very few Moms accepted the fact that they control their kids but gradually when we discuss more on this topic, few of them accepted the fact and said, "Sometimes we control our kids but for their benefit."

Maharashtra based Educator Sana Inamdar said, "No, my child knows his boundaries and sometimes he is cranky but I talk to him and everything get sought out."

The degree of control Moms exert over their children varies depending on parenting styles, cultural norms, and individual family dynamics. While Moms have authority and responsibility for guiding and supervising their children, the concept of "control" can be nuanced.

In some families, Moms may employ authoritative parenting, which involves setting clear expectations and boundaries while also being responsive and nurturing. In this approach, Moms guide their children's behavior through positive reinforcement, communication, and mutual respect rather than strict control.

On the other hand, some Moms may adopt authoritarian parenting, characterized by strict rules, punishment, and little room for negotiation. While this approach may involve a high level of control, it can also lead to strained mother child relationships and hinder the development of autonomy and critical thinking skills in children.

Further, we came to the conclusion that the reasons for this 'control' may vary from parent to parent; a few reasons are mentioned below:

1. Not having enough trust in their abilities

2. Unwillingness to let go of taking care of their kids

3. Fear of losing them

4. Trying to raise them as perfect and ideal

5. Afraid they might make any wrong mistakes like they did in the past.

Ultimately, effective parenting involves finding a balance between control and autonomy, allowing children to develop independence while providing guidance and support along the way. It's essential for Moms to consider their children's individual needs, personalities, and developmental stages when determining the appropriate level of control in parenting.

15 | Do Mothers Have Their Favorite Kids?

First, it could be biologically driven. When a parent holds their newborn baby, they typically experience a flood of hormones that create a strong attachment and bond with their child. This bond may be further reinforced as the parent sees their child grow and develop.

Obviously, no mom will accept that they have a favorite kid, as they treat them equally like me. I have two sons with an age gap of 2 years; whenever they ask who is your favorite child, I always tell them you both are like my two hands. Can I cut one? After that, I need not to say anything. As expected, I got the same answer from all Moms.

This was a universal fact until I came across a psychologist mom who busted my myth; she explained the term with logic and said,

"Parents tend to favor a child that is most like them, reminds them of themselves, or represents what they view as a success of parenting."

She said, "Usually, we as Moms are always inclined towards the weak child or the child who needs more attention."

She further explained. "Younger children are most likely to have been raised by a parent who is experienced, more confident and skilled in terms of child-raising."

16│Is Yelling Right?

The ideal answer to this question is "No" in any condition but practically this question is a topic of debate between Moms. 70 % of Moms from Gen X and Y believe that sometimes they have to use this technique to control their actions but whereas 80% of Gen Z moms are against yelling.

The use of yelling as a form of discipline or communication. While every parent's approach to parenting may differ, it's important to consider the impact of yelling on our children and our relationships with them.

Our research shows that yelling and harsh verbal discipline can have similar negative effects as corporal punishment. Children who are constantly yelled at are more likely to have behavioral problems, anxiety, depression, stress, and other emotional issues, similar to children who are hit or spanked frequently.

Yelling can be a natural response to frustration or stress, but it's essential to recognise its potential consequences. Yelling can create an atmosphere of fear, erode trust, and damage our children's self-esteem. Instead of fostering understanding and cooperation, it may lead to resentment and communication barriers.

As Moms, we play a crucial role in shaping our children's emotional well-being and behavior. While we may feel overwhelmed at times, it's important to find healthy ways to manage our emotions and communicate with our children effectively. This may involve practicing patience, active listening, and setting clear boundaries.

Let's strive to create a nurturing and supportive environment for our children where open communication and mutual respect are valued. By modelling positive behavior and using constructive discipline strategies, we can foster a strong and loving relationship with our children that lasts a lifetime.

17 | Why Are There so Many Parenting Approaches That Are Famous Nowadays?

Nowadays, when everyone is so concerned about their child's growth and overall development, they try to balance their physical, mental, and emotional growth too. There are several reasons why different parenting approaches are popular nowadays, a few of them are mentioned below:

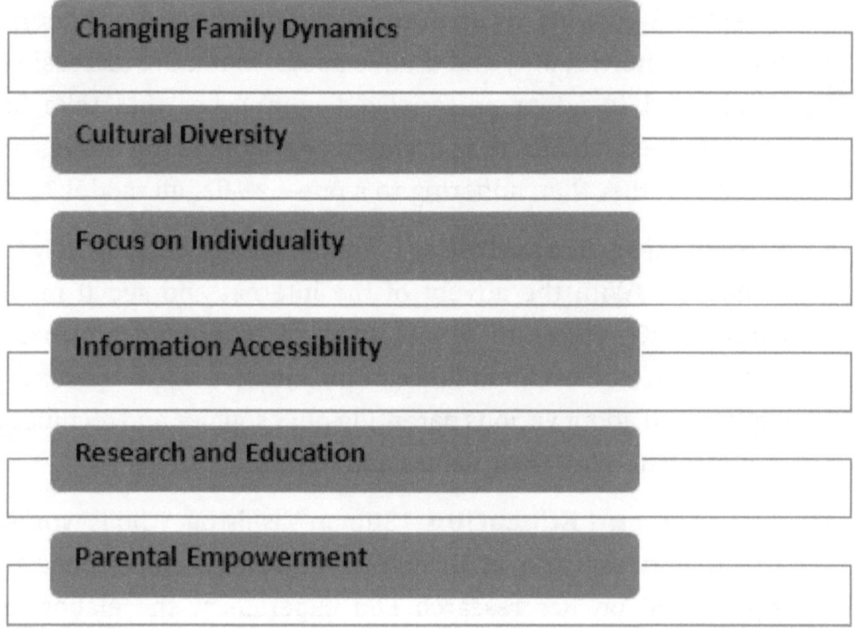

- **Changing Family Dynamics** – One of the famous politician Moms shared, while she meet different kind of people every day, over the time she discovered, "Family structures have evolved over time, leading to diverse parenting approaches tailored to different family compositions, such as single-parent households, blended families, same-sex parents, and co-parenting arrangements. Each family dynamic may require a different approach to parenting."

- **Cultural Diversity** – A mom working in government sector on a higher post shared her view on this topic, She elaborated, "As societies become more diverse, parenting approaches are influenced by cultural norms, traditions, and practices from around the world. Parents may draw from different cultural perspectives to create a unique parenting style that reflects their heritage and experiences."

- **Focus on Individuality** – Jodhpur based Dr. Nidhi Jain said, "There is a growing recognition of the importance of honoring children's individuality and unique needs. Moms are increasingly encouraged to adopt personalized approaches that take into account their child's temperament, developmental stage, and interests rather than adhering to a one-size-fits-all model."

- **Information Accessibility** – Shilpa, who is working in MNC, explained, "With the advent of the internet and social media, parents have access to a vast array of parenting information and resources. This abundance of information allows parents to explore and adopt various parenting philosophies and techniques that resonate with their values and beliefs."

- **Research and Education** – Suman Vashistha, who is working as A deputy registrar at Gurugram University, enlightened this topic based on her research and experience; she elaborated, "Over the span of time, psychology, neuroscience, and child development research have provided valuable insights into effective parenting practices." According to her, "Parents are more informed about the impact of their parenting choices on their children's long-term well-being and are therefore more willing to explore and adapt their approaches based on scientific evidence."

- **Parental Empowerment** – Poorva Chaturvedi, A banker Mom from Gurugram said, "Modern parents are empowered to make informed decisions about their parenting style and approach. They are encouraged to trust their instincts, seek support from parenting communities, and priorities their own well-being as they navigate the challenges of raising children in today's world."

As per the above discussion from Moms working in different industries, I can conclude the diversity of parenting approaches reflects the evolving nature of parenting in response to societal changes, cultural influences, and a growing body of knowledge about child development and psychology.

18 | Different Moms - Different Parenting Approaches

After knowing the reason and importance of choosing different parenting approaches, let's take a few examples of 21st century's parenting approaches. (Disclaimer: few of the approaches are taken by google to enhance the topic)

1. ABC Approach

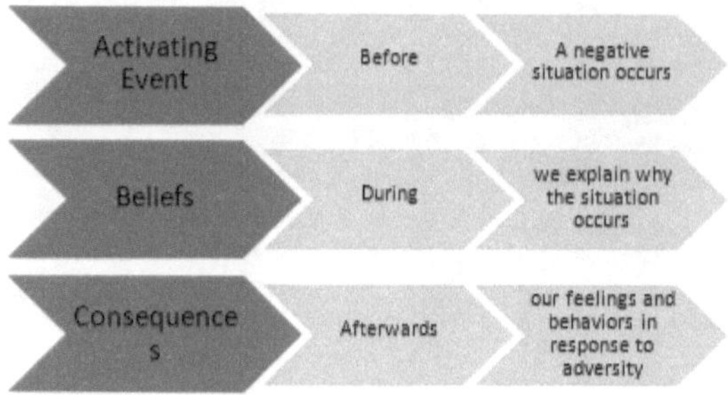

The ABCs of behavior will help Moms to know how to best teach their children new behaviors. Children move through behaviors in three stages: Activating Event (before), Behavior/Beliefs (during), and consequences (afterwards). Children can change their behaviors during any of these stages, but the approach is the same.

2. Four C's

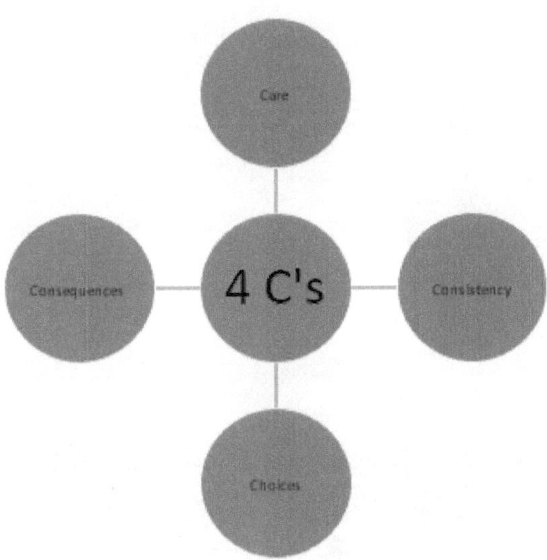

This approach is significance in how Moms can support children with a foundation of love, care, and consistency, giving them choices and telling them the consequences of any event or problem.

3. 5 Essentials/Pillars of Parenting

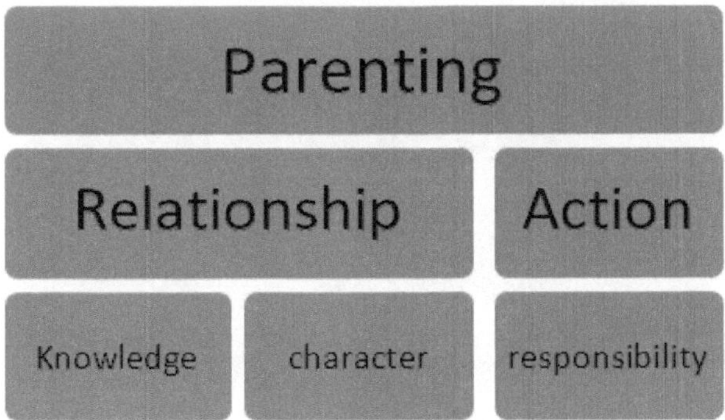

If, as a mom, you want to rebuild your relationship with your kids, you may follow this approach, which is the blend of a few essentials like Your actions + Responsibility + Creating good character + Giving enough knowledge + strengthening your relationships.

4. 5'c of Parenting

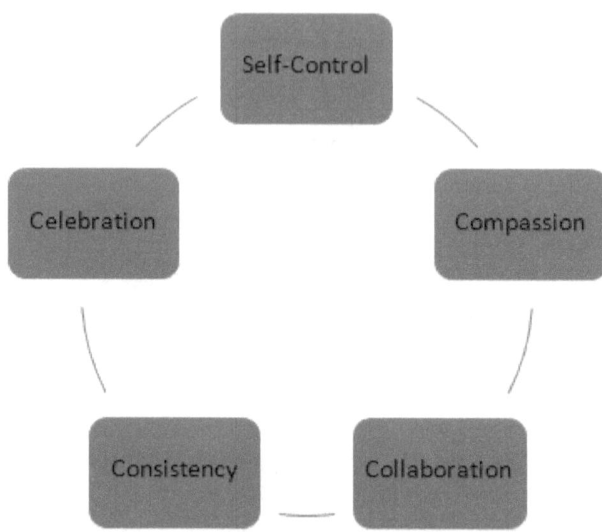

Moms, if you would like to encourage a growth mindset where effort and progress are celebrated over perfection. Saline's five C's of ADHD parenting—self-control, compassion, collaboration, consistency, and celebration—provide a comprehensive guide for nurturing success in your child's life.

5. 4 Styles of parenting

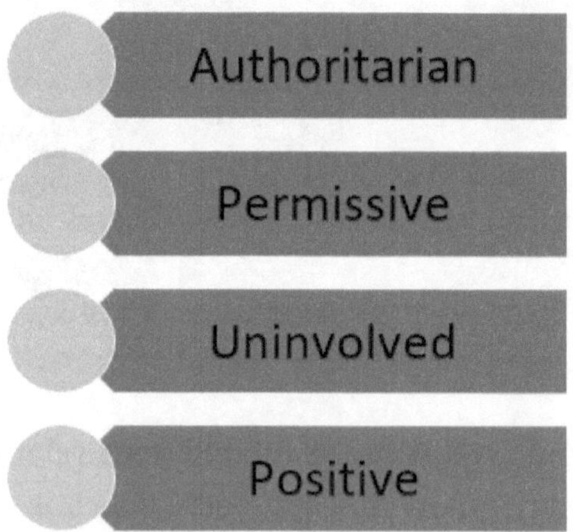

Moms, there are four main styles of parenting – authoritarian, permissive, uninvolved and positive parenting. Most parents have a style they naturally favor; it's very common to move between four types depending on your circumstances and mood at the time.

6. 3 F's of Parenting

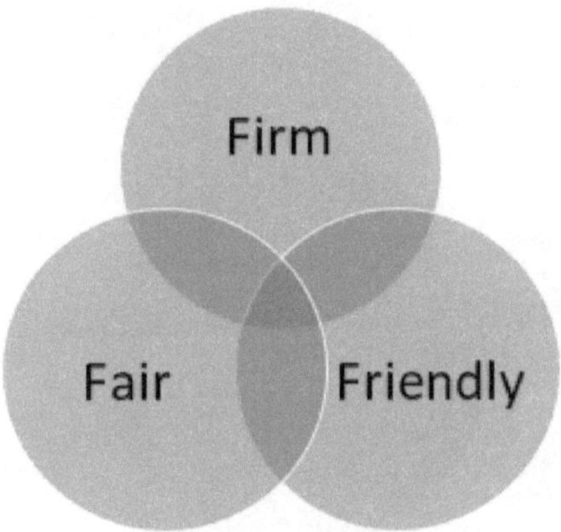

Dear Moms, here is the coolest parenting approach and also proved an effective parenting style popular among most of the youngest generation's Moms' firm + fair + friendly

7. Bare Minimum Parenting

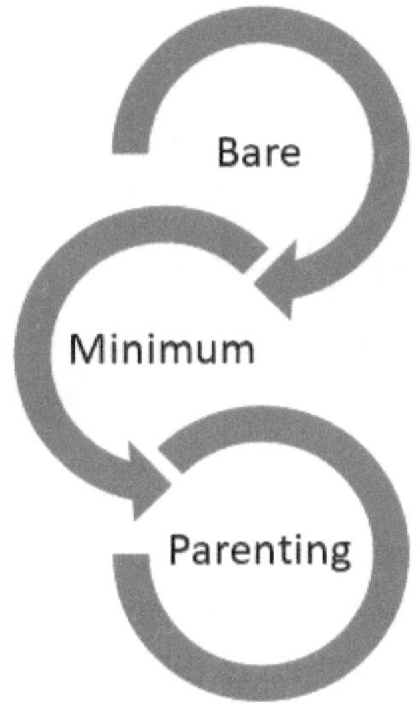

Moms, this parenting approach will turn your child into a functional adult with only a fraction of the effort spent by super Moms. If you do it right, your kid will be no better or worse off than their kids, but with more free time left for you.

8. Tough Love Parenting

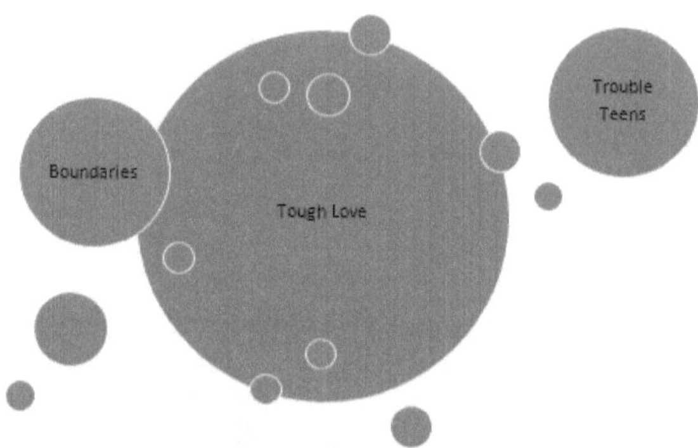

Moms, if you are dealing with teenage kids, you may opt for this approach for the short term. It is defined as setting clear boundaries and limits with enforced consequences and is most often used with troubled teens. Generally speaking, is this effective parenting in the short term but not in the long run?

9. Lazy Parenting Style

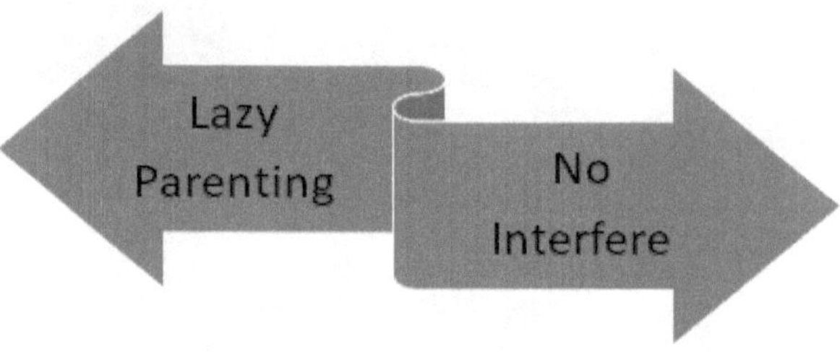

Dear Moms, Lazy parenting is a type of parenting where a mom consciously withholds herself from interfering in everything the child does. The mom allows the child to do day-to-day tasks on their own, so that the child gains confidence in doing things. The child is allowed to make mistakes and learn from them.

10. Neglectful Parenting

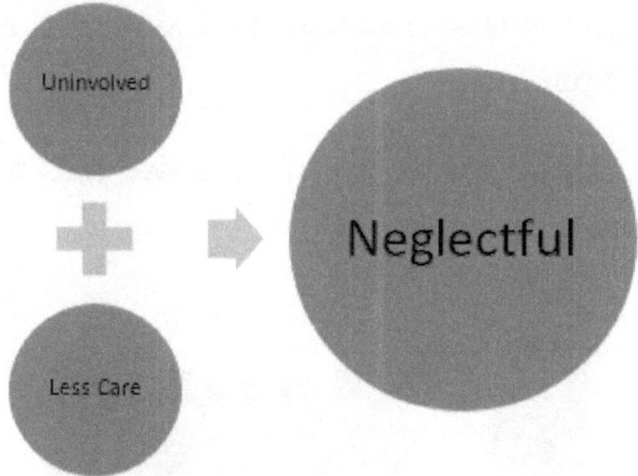

According to parenting experts across the globe believes that, this is one of the worst parenting styles,. Not only does it promote leaving kids to fend for themselves, but it also offers much less care and engagement with them. Uninvolved or neglectful parenting is considered the most damaging for a child's development due to the lack of consistency, warmth, nurturing, and support and the child develop as hyper-independence as an adult.

11. Toxic Parenting

When people discuss toxic parents, they are typically describing parents who consistently behave in ways that cause guilt, fear, or obligation in their children. Their actions aren't isolated events but patterns of behavior that negatively shape their child's life. The name that is sometimes used to describe a child brought up by toxic parents is a "scapegoat." This term refers to a child who is unfairly blamed or targeted for the problems and dysfunction within the family, often by toxic or narcissistic parents.

12. Authoritarian, Authoritative and Permissive parenting approach by Psychologist Diana Baumrind

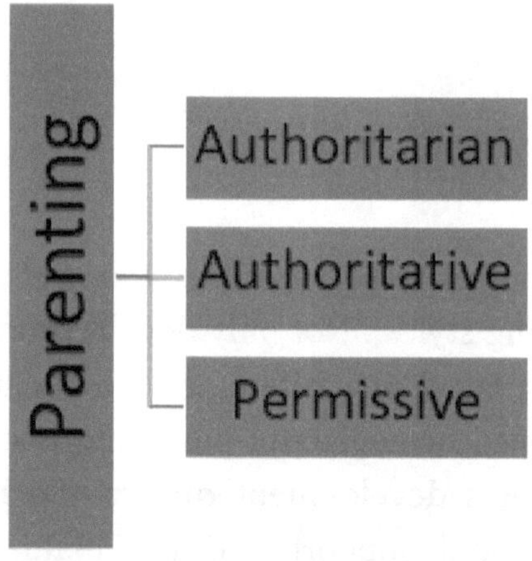

Psychologist Diana Baumrind's Theory of Parenting

According to Psychologist Diana Baumrind, **Authoritarian parenting** is marked by strict rules and high demands with no flexibility. Parents expect unquestioning obedience from their children and enforce rules. Communication tends to be one-way, with limited room for negotiation or discussion. While this style may lead to immediate compliance, it can also result in children feeling anxious, rebellious, or lacking in self-esteem due to the lack of warmth and autonomy.

Whereas if we talk about **authoritative parenting**, It's characterized by a balance of warmth and discipline. Parents set clear expectations and rules but also provide support and understanding. They value independence and encourage open communication with their children. This style fosters self-discipline, responsibility, and emotional maturity in children, leading to positive outcomes in their social, academic, and emotional development.

But if we talk about **permissive parenting**, it involves high levels of warmth and support but minimal structure and discipline. Parents in this style tend to be lenient in setting firm boundaries or enforcing rules. They priorities their children's happiness and freedom over obedience or self-control. While children raised in permissive households may feel loved and valued, they can struggle with self-discipline, boundaries, and decision-making skills, potentially leading to challenges in their behavior and relationships later in life.

19 | Today's Kids

(late Gen Z & Gen Alpha)

Just like we have three generations of Moms right now, Do you know which generation we are raising today, Confused?

Dear Moms, according to United Nations Population Fund's (UNFPA) State of world population -2024 report, In India population below 14 is 24%, 10-19 are 17% (who consider non-adults) and between 10-24 is 26%, So whether you are raising fussy teen or Adolescent or kids or toddlers or Infants this research is for you.

Today's kids either belong to Gen Z or Gen Alpha. 80% of the mothers in this research are raising these two generations. Let's find out about them in detail:

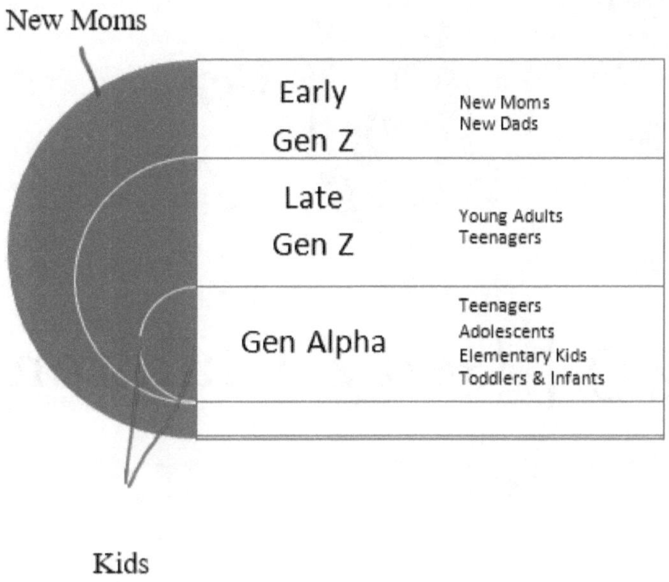

New Moms
Kids
Early
Gen Z
New Moms
New Dads
Late
Gen Z
Young Adults
Teenagers
Gen Alpha
Teenagers
Adolescents
Elementary Kids
Toddlers & Infants

20 | Gen Z Children

Generation Z kids, born roughly between the mid-1990s and early 2010s, exhibit a range of characteristics shaped by their upbringing, societal influences, and technological advancements. Although we have already read about them under Gen Z Moms, the late Gen Z, who are still in their teens, need to be studied. Our expert Moms tell us about how Gen Z differs from previous generations; here, we customize their answers for you:

How late Gen Z kids are different?	Digital Natives
	Entrepreneurial Spirit
	Diverse and Inclusive
	Information Access
	Socially Conscious
	Flexible and Adaptable
	Social Media Influencers
	Socially Conscious
	Desire for Authenticity

- **Digital Natives** – Banker Mom Poorva Chaturvedi said, "Unlike our generations, who experienced the rise of technology, These small little wonders have grown up with it. They are digital natives who have been comfortable with smartphones, social media, and the internet from a young age. This innate familiarity shapes their communication, learning, and social interactions in ways that previous generations might not fully understand."

- **Entrepreneurial Spirit** – Recently in newspapers and social media we have seen numbers of examples Teen Entrepreneurs. I have seen teen authors also, who are not only doing studies and sports but they are more into business and app development. They have entrepreneurial mindset. They are more likely to start their own businesses or pursue independent ventures at a young age, leveraging technology and social media to promote their ideas and products.

- **Diverse and Inclusive** – When I last visited Vrindavan, I saw many young children from India and abroad who were taking knowledge at Gurukul. I personally believe that although they are modern, they want to rejoin the roots of our culture. They are the most diverse generation yet, both ethnically and culturally. They embrace diversity and inclusivity as fundamental values, advocating for representation and equality across various aspects of society.

- **Information Access** - With access to vast amounts of information online, Gen Z is highly informed and critical thinkers. They are less likely to passively accept information and more inclined to fact-check and verify sources. They check the facts first and then rely on them. My younger brother, who is a music producer by profession, always gives me 1000 tips on how to use modern technology, and I always wonder how backwards we are. It's funny but true; let me tell you, he belongs to Gen Z.

- **Flexible and Adaptable** - Growing up in a rapidly changing world, Generation Z is adaptable and flexible. They are accustomed to constant innovation and disruption, which can translate into a willingness to embrace change and take risks. According to a report 80% of Bitcoin users belongs to Gen Z.

- **Social Media Influencers** - Gen Z kids value individuality and self-expression, often using social media as a platform to showcase their creativity, opinions, and personal style.

- **Socially Conscious** - Generation Z is deeply concerned about social and environmental issues. They are more politically active and socially engaged than previous generations, using their voices to advocate for change on topics such as climate change, gun control, human rights, motivational stories, social work, sharing and caring, etc. Many of my friend's kids and mine too are working on this through their YouTube channels.

- **Desire for Authenticity** - Gen Z values authenticity in brands, influencers, and public figures. They are sceptical of traditional advertising and respond positively to genuine, transparent communication.

We came on conclusion that, Gen Z's upbringing in a digital, diverse, and socially conscious world has shaped them into a generation with distinct values, behaviors, and attitudes as compare to their previous generations.

Challenges Gen Z faces

Despite so many achievements in terms of the most digitally active and socially aware generation. These kids also face challenges in balancing their digital lives with their appreciation for nature. We are as Gen Y, are the sandwich between Gen X and Gen Z, so we are also connected to them personally, I have my niece and nephews, friends' kids from this particular Gen Z, and I personally spoke to them on this topic.

According to Vanshika Bharadwaj, who herself is a teenager elaborated this topic with few of her friends for us, I hope every teenager can relate with them and every Mom and Dad may understand what they want.

She said, It's my growing phase, in which I also discover many new things about myself and the world. The challenges I faced while making a bond with my parents were -

Challenges of Gen Z kids	Less Independence of decision making
	Generation Gap
	No Open Communication
	High Expectations
	Fear of How Will They React
	Crushes and Love
	Short Attention Span
	Excess Screen Time
	Financial Uncertainty
	Mental Health
	Education Disruption
	Physical Health
	Struggle to maintain life style
	Less Face to Face Interaction
	Political Divisiveness
	Climate Change

- **Less Independence of Decision-Making** - I feel like parents give less independence in decision-making to their teenagers. Giving teenagers independence in decision-making is very crucial for their development into responsible adults.

- **Generation Gap** - There is a huge generation gap between teenagers and their parents. Teenagers and parents hold different values and beliefs and also different attitude towards things due to growing up in different eras which creates misunderstandings.

- **No Open Communication** - many teenage friends and I feel uncomfortable communicating openly with our parents about feelings.

- **High Expectations** - There are high expectations of parents from their teenagers, such as high expectations of performing well in academics and ideal mode of behavior.

- **Fear of How Will They React** - I struggle to express my feelings to my parents which leads to lack of emotional connection and trust with them, so I share my feelings to my friends instead.

- **Crushes and Love**: Teenagers fear telling their parents about their crush or romantic relationship due to fear, judgement, parental rules or the fear of disappointing their parents and fear of how their parents will react. It's a mix of wanting to tell their parents about it and hiding it.

- Further, I spoke to a psychologist who has been handling teenagers for the last five years. She elaborated on the topic for all the parents who are handling these teens:

- **Short Attention Span** – According to her, "Due to the constant influx of information and stimulation from the internet and social media, Gen Z kids may have shorter attention spans and a preference for bite-sized content that can be consumed quickly."

- **Excess Screen Time and social media usage** – It can sometimes hinder their connection to the natural world. With the rise of smartphones and social media, They are often glued to screens, leading to concerns about addiction.

- **Financial Uncertainty** - Many of them are entering adulthood during a time of economic uncertainty, with issues like student loan debt, rising housing costs, and job market instability affecting their prospects for the future. While witnessing the financial struggles of previous generations, prioritizing savings, budgeting, and financial literacy. They are always busy adjusting to their financial needs.

- **Mental Health** – I have seen many teenagers leading to concerns about their mental and physical well-being. Higher rates of mental health issues such as anxiety and depression are often exacerbated by societal pressures, academic stress, and the constant comparison fostered by social media.

- **Education Disruption** - The COVID-19 pandemic has disrupted education for Gen Z kids, leading to challenges with remote learning, academic achievement gaps, and uncertainty about the future of their education.

- **Physical Health** – As compare to previous generations they are less active in sports and any other physical activity. Which leads to health issues in future.

- **Struggle to maintain lifestyle** – They struggle with the disconnect between their desire for a sustainable lifestyle and convenience-driven habits, which are ingrained in modern society.

- **Less Face-to-Face Interaction** – As per few known, They are not willing to join social get together or don't like to sit in groups with other generations, instead you may find them active on social media.

- **Political Divisiveness** - Growing up in a politically polarized world, Gen Z kids face challenges in navigating divisive political discourse and finding common ground with those who hold opposing views.

- **Climate Change** – They are growing up in a world increasingly affected by climate change. They face the daunting task of mitigating its effects while also demanding action from older generations and institutions.

Tips for Teenagers

Teenager Vanshika shared a few tips, which she tried to make a good relationship with her parents –

- **Being Patient** - I tried being patient with them, listening to them and understanding their concerns for me.

- **Quality Time** - I spend quality time with my parents and do activities we both enjoy, such as watching a movie together.

- **Make Myself Better** - I try to make myself better and study well.

- **Complementing and making them feel loved** - I compliment my parents like "you're looking good today" and hugging or kissing them.

She concluded the whole scenario and said, "Parents always want their children to be happy and successful. It's just different styles of parenting and different attitudes towards things which create conflicts between them." Kudos to the thoughtfulness of Vanshika Bharadwaj. Best of luck to her for future.

Finally, Despite these challenges, Gen Z is known for its resilience, activism, and determination to create positive change in the world. They are actively working to address these issues and shape a better future for themselves and generations to come.

Before taking about Gen Alpha, let me first tell you about the difference between Gen Z and Alpha.

Generation Alpha, born from around 2010 onwards, share some similarities with Gen Z but also have notable differences:

Gen Z and Gen Alpha Similarities V/S Differences	
	Junior Milliners
	Technology Integration
	Cultural Influences
	Educational Trends
	Diverse Family Structures
	Environmental Consciousness
	Global Awareness

- **Junior Milliners** – Yes! You read right; the junior milliners is the new term. They are influencers, they are YouTubers, and they have been doing modelling since day one. And now they are milliners. Compared to Gen Z, they have many more opportunities because their parents belong to the youngest generation of society.

- **Technology Integration** - While Generation Z grew up in a digital world, Generation Alpha is growing up in an even more technologically advanced environment. For Generation Alpha, technology is even more seamlessly integrated into their lives, with the proliferation of smart devices, artificial intelligence, and virtual reality shaping their experiences from birth.

- **Cultural Influences** - Generation Alpha will be influenced by a new wave of cultural trends, media, and entertainment. As they come of age, they will shape and redefine cultural norms, preferences, and forms of expression in ways that may differ from Generation Z.

- **Educational Trends** - Generation Alpha is likely to experience further shifts in education, with a greater emphasis on technology integration, personalized learning, and digital literacy. They may have different learning styles and preferences compared to Generation Z, necessitating adjustments in educational approaches.

- **Diverse Family Structures** - Generation Alpha is experiencing a wider range of family structures, including more blended families, same-sex parents, and single-parent households. This diversity in family dynamics may influence their perspectives on relationships, identity, and social norms.

- **Environmental Consciousness** - While Generation Z is already known for its environmental activism, Generation Alpha may be even more environmentally conscious. Growing up in a world facing urgent environmental challenges, they may priorities sustainability and eco-friendly practices from an early age.

- **Global Awareness** - Generation Alpha is growing up in an increasingly interconnected world, with access to global information and cultures from a young age. They may have a broader understanding of global issues and a more global perspective compared to Generation Z.

21 | Generation Alpha

(The Youngest Generation on Earth)

What Is ALPHA?

"Alpha mode" typically refers to a state of being assertive, confident, and proactive. In the context of parenting or caregiving, it can mean taking charge and leading with authority while providing guidance and support to children. In context to alpha kids, the kids born between 2010 and 2025 are known to be alpha kids with assertive, confident and proactive natures.

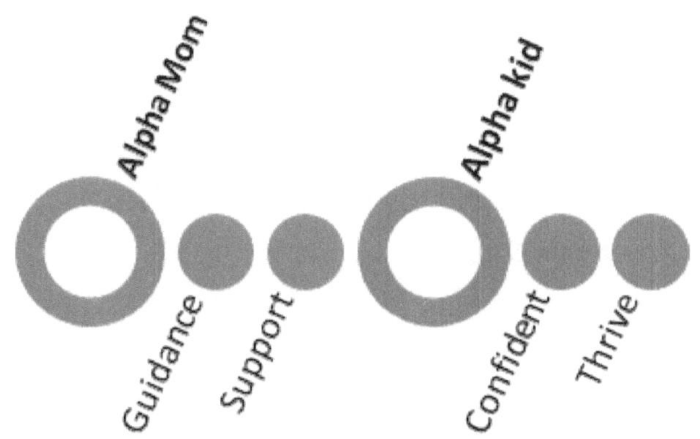

The difference between an alpha mom and an alpha kid lies in their roles, responsibilities, and stages of development:

Alpha Moms

- Alpha Moms priorities their children's well-being and development, advocating for their needs and interests while fostering independence and responsibility.

- They are assertive, proactive caregivers who take charge of parenting responsibilities with confidence and authority.

- They set boundaries, provide guidance, and lead by example in raising their children.

- They play a central role in shaping their children's values, behaviors, and life skills through consistent guidance, support, and discipline.

Alpha Kid

- An alpha kid contains leadership qualities, strong opinions, and a drive to take initiative in various aspects of their lives.

- They exhibit assertive, confident, and independent traits from a young age.

- They challenge authority, question rules, and seek autonomy in decision-making, often displaying a high level of energy and assertiveness.

- They thrive in environments that offer opportunities for exploration, problem-solving, and personal growth, but they may also require guidance and support in managing their assertiveness and channeling their energy effectively.

Are You in Alpha Mode or Dependent Mode?

There are two sets of instincts: The "alpha mode" and the other is The "dependent mode."

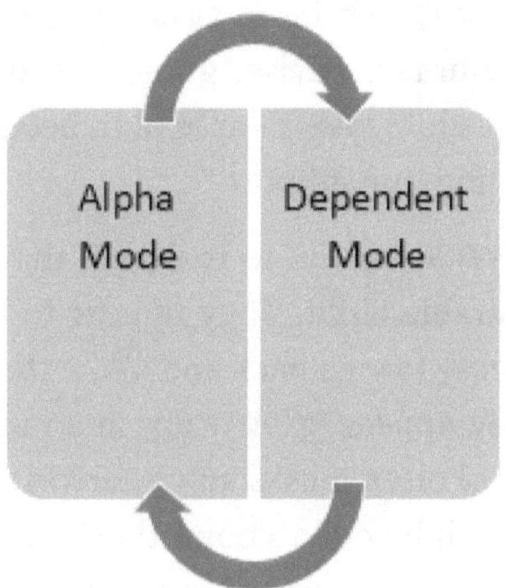

As Moms, we generally take turns with our partner taking the alpha or the dependent mode depending on the context, but in a parent-child relationship, usually, the parent is in the alpha mode, and the child is in the dependent mode. Sometimes, this gets turned on its head, and the child ends up in alpha mode, with the parent wondering how they lost their lead. A Parenting expert mom says, "A child who operates in the alpha mode most of the time is called an alpha child."

Is There Anything Wrong In ALPHA?

There's nothing "wrong" with alpha instincts. They are an important and instinctive part of every single one of us. However, the alpha mode is healthiest in the context of caring for others. To be healthy, the drive to take charge should always be accompanied by a drive to assume responsibility for and care for others, giving the one in the alpha mode the position that is best for providing for and protecting others.

A child who has taken the alpha mode in the parent-child relationship has the drive to take charge, but it is not usually accompanied by the drive to take responsibility for nor to care for others. Alpha children can be very difficult to take care of. They can be bossy, controlling and demanding. They resist instruction or direction, must be in the know all the time and are driven to take center stage.

A leading Parenting Coach Mom says, "As parents, it is our job to support, care for, encourage, advise, guide and direct our children as they develop. An alpha child uses their lead to become the one advising, directing and demanding our support."

She elaborated, "What we fail to realize is that a child in the alpha mode is often a vulnerable child. They appear to be strong, confident, and in control, so it's easy to step back and allow them to make their own decisions because they appear 'grown up' in so many ways. However, the drive to take control often masks an underlying sense of anxiety and alarm. Deep down, an alpha child knows they're not quite ready for the responsibilities of the adult world. As Moms, it's our responsibility to use our instincts to resolve problems."

WHY IS MY CHILD ALPHA?

During my conversation with a group of Moms in club, one of the Moms was disagree with the theory of alpha child and started giving examples that the kids are not disciplined and need to change by hook or crook, then one of expert in child psychology took charge and clarified our doubts, she further explained, She has given this theory as "2D of alpha" There are two reasons why the child is alpha?

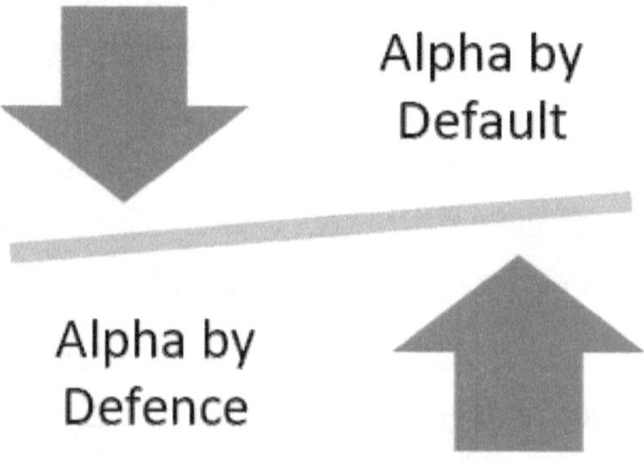

- **Alpha by Default**

  A child can become alpha "by default." This means the parent has not taken a firm lead in their relationship with the child, creating a gap for the child to step in to. This situation can be created for many reasons, such as by overly casual or permissive parenting. It could be because the parent is overly anxious or uncertain. It could be because the parent believes in creating an equal status between parent and child, possibly because their own parent was overly dominating. It could also be because of the joint family, where parents can't make the decision alone.

- **Alpha by Defence**

  A child can also become alpha "by Defence." The child's parents may be operating in alpha mode, but it still doesn't feel safe for the child to depend upon them. This could be because a child feels let down by their parent in a frightening situation, or it could be because the child experiences a sense that their parent is taking advantage of their weakness or making fun of them. These contexts can trigger a Defence in the child against vulnerable feelings such as caring – a vital part of a healthy alpha expression.

  As a result, the child's limbic brain chooses the alpha mode as the only safe mode to operate in.

Are Alpha Kids Difficult to Handle?

Labelling any generation as "the most difficult" is subjective and can be misleading. Each generation faces its own set of challenges and complexities. However, there are several factors that could potentially make Gen Alpha challenging to understand and engage with.

Challenges among Alpha kids	Short Attention Span
	Digitally Overloaded
	Cybersecurity Risks
	Digital Addiction
	Educational Pressure
	ABCD factor Alpha-Bossy-Controlling-Demanding
	Social Skills Development
	Changing Family Dynamics
	Lack of Physical Activity
	Education Transformation
	Mental Health Concerns
	Uncertain Career Landscape
	Environmental Concerns

- **Attention Span** - Constant access to information may reduce attention spans and hinder their ability to focus on tasks for extended periods.

- **Digitally Overloaded** - With constant exposure to digital devices and screens, there's a risk of information overload, reduced attention spans, and potential negative impacts on learning skills.

- **Cybersecurity Risks** - Growing up in a digital world makes them vulnerable to online threats such as cyberbullying, identity theft, and online predators. Exposure to the internet from a young age poses risks such as inappropriate content consumption.

- **Digital Addiction** - Excessive screen time and reliance on digital devices can lead to addiction, affecting their mental and physical health.

- **Educational Pressure** - The pressure to excel academically in a competitive global landscape, coupled with the fast-paced nature of technological advancements, can create stress and anxiety among Generation Alpha students.

- **ABCD factor Alpha-Bossy-Controlling-Demanding** - They can be very difficult to take care of. They can be bossy, controlling and demanding. They resist instruction or direction and are driven to take center stage.

- **Social Skills Development** - Despite being highly connected digitally, Gen Alpha may face challenges in developing strong interpersonal and communication skills necessary for meaningful relationships and collaboration in the offline world.

- **Changing Family Dynamics** - Generation Alpha is experiencing diverse family structures, which can present unique challenges related to identity, relationships, and social norms. Adapting to non-traditional family setups may require greater support and understanding from caregivers and society.

- **Lack of Physical Activity** - Increased screen time and sedentary lifestyles can contribute to health issues such as obesity, poor posture, and decreased physical fitness.

- **Education Transformation** - The education system is undergoing rapid transformation, with a greater emphasis on technology integration, personalized learning, and digital literacy. Adapting to these changes and ensuring that educational approaches meet the diverse needs of Generation Alpha learners may present challenges for educators and policymakers.

- **Mental Health Concerns** - Like previous generations, Generation Alpha may face mental health challenges such as anxiety, depression, and social isolation. Addressing these concerns and providing adequate support and resources for mental well-being will be crucial in fostering their overall development.

- **Uncertain career Landscape** - Rapid automation and technological disruption may reshape the job market by the time Generation Alpha enters the workforce, requiring them to adapt to new skills and career paths.

- **Environmental Concerns** - As awareness of environmental issues grows, Generation Alpha may feel the weight of addressing climate change and sustainability concerns inherited from previous generations.

While addressing these problems, Jodhpur based Dr. Nidhi Jain, who herself is handelling two alpha kids clarifies, "We Moms require a balanced approach that leverages the benefits of technology while mitigating its negative effects, along with promoting holistic development and environmental consciousness from an early age." She further elaborated, "While Generation Alpha may encounter unique challenges, it's essential to approach them with understanding, empathy, and support rather than labelling them as inherently difficult. By recognizing and addressing the specific needs and circumstances of this generation, we can better prepare them to navigate the complexities of the modern world."

22 | What Happens When the Child Is Not Raised Properly in a Positive Environment

According to few doctor Moms, I know that this issue is not a small one; one negative seed can raise a toxic adult, which leads to another toxic family, and this will become a never-ending toxic cycle. They further explain, "When a child is raised in a negative environment, they may experience a range of negative consequences that can impact their emotional, psychological, and social well-being."

Suman Vashistha, who has done counselling for these kind of adults during the last one year under Mission Purple, elaborated this topic by dividing the whole pattern into five levels, which are mentioned below:

<table>
<tr><td>1st</td><td>Emotional Dysregulation
Difficulty Trusting Others</td></tr>
<tr><td>2nd</td><td>Start finding role model outside or vise versa
Impaired Social Skills</td></tr>
<tr><td>3rd</td><td>Codependency
Difficulty Establishing Boundaries</td></tr>
<tr><td>4th</td><td>Low Self-Esteem
Anxiety and Depression</td></tr>
<tr><td>5th</td><td>Perpetuating Toxic Patterns</td></tr>
</table>

Level 1 – According to her, when a child doesn't get enough support from close family members, especially Moms and regular exposure to chronic stress, emotional volatility, or neglections can impair a child's ability to regulate their emotions effectively, leading to mood swings, outbursts, or difficulty coping with stress later in his/her life. Growing up in an environment where trust is undermined or betrayed can make it difficult for children to trust others too.

Level 2 – When they have no trust at home they started finding it outside or they become totally anti-social. They may struggle with social skills and forming healthy relationships, as they may not have had positive role models or opportunities to learn effective communication and conflict resolution skills.

Level 3 – Sometimes, these kinds of children may develop codependent tendencies, feeling responsible for their parents' emotions or behaviors and sacrificing their own needs to maintain the relationship. Which is a very harsh reality to accept. They may also disregard their child's boundaries or fail to model healthy boundaries themselves, making it challenging for the child to establish and maintain boundaries in their own relationships.

Level 4 - Constant criticism, belittling, or invalidation from parents can erode a child's self-esteem and confidence, leading to feelings of worthlessness or inadequacy. Living in this kind of environment characterized by conflict, unpredictability, or emotional abuse can contribute to the development of anxiety and depression in children at very young ages.

Level 5 – Finally, without intervention or support, children raised in a negative environment may unknowingly perpetuate toxic behaviors and relationship patterns in their own adult lives, continuing the cycle of dysfunction.

Although, she believes that the impact of a negative environment can vary widely depending on factors such as the severity and duration of the negativity, the child's individual temperament, and the presence of supportive relationships or interventions. However, seeking therapy, building a supportive network, and cultivating self-awareness can help individuals who have been raised in a negative environment to heal and break free from harmful patterns.

At the end of this topic, I would like to suggest something on my personal behalf. Dear Moms, choose your words wisely and take care of the environment in which we are raising our children. Sometimes, we have to raise our voices not for our sake but for the flowers which are blooming in our garden; healthy environment and healthy habits are their fundamental right, which should be taken care of. Although there's a saying that we need a village to raise a kid perfectly for our little lovely kids, we are the village. Remember, if you didn't stand for yourself, at least take a stand for your kid.

23 | Why Kids Start Ignoring Their Moms?

According to my research, many Moms accepted the fact that after a certain age, their kids start ignoring them; after detailed analysis, I found that there are certain situations when the kids start misbehaving or, at last, start ignoring their Moms. A few of them are mentioned below:

1. Unresolved Emotional Strain
2. Seeking independence
3. Testing boundaries
4. Differences in values
5. Conflicts over past events
6. Parental conflict
7. Stress at school
8. Feel misunderstood
9. Changes in the family dynamic
10. New sibling

These strained emotions and conflicts can lead to stress, anxiety, and relationship issues for both mom and kid.

24 | Tips to Resolve These Issues

As we diagnose the problem now, we should talk about resolving the issue in an effective way. One of the leading parenting experts and Coordinator of a famous Montessori school in Gurugram suggested a few tips to resolve this issue:

1. Effective Communication Between Mom And Child

2. Moms can create opportunities for open dialogue.

3. Actively listen to their child's concerns.

4. Validate their feelings

5. Spending quality time together

6. Engaging in activities that both enjoy

7. Setting clear and reasonable expectations

8. Consistent behavior in resolving conflicts

9. Establish healthy boundaries while still fostering a nurturing and supportive relationship.

10. Showing genuine interest in their child's life can help strengthen the bond and reduce the likelihood of ignoring behaviors.

So, Moms, try to implement the points I shared and feel the difference by yourself.

25 | How to Tackle Alpha Kids?

Digital Marketing expert mom Prachi Kalra said, "Parenting is hard. Possibly the most underrated sentence of the century – but it's true. Parents have the task of raising children – teaching them right from wrong, how to tie their shoes, how to be a good sportsperson, how to deal with heartbreak and everything in between. We also know that children are sponges and begin soaking up lessons before we realize we're even giving them."

While many children don't remember the first few years of their lives, the moments and memories they do remember can stick with them into adulthood. Because of that, a parent's behavior in the home can have a lasting impact on children, as preschoolers and beyond.

Parenting trends are just that – trends. Millennial Moms are raising their children differently from their upbringing. New information and new technology have taught us that children between the ages of 2-5 should have no more than an hour of screen time each day. But, while there is no magic formula for how to parent. Maybe it's time to remind everyone once again that parenting is hard. While everyone has their own style, we have one key piece of information that can potentially help parents raise successful children – emotional support, beginning at an early age.

We may all still be trying to figure out what parenting style is right for our families and children, but in the meantime, we can offer the support our children need to lead successful lives.

Children are growing up in such a different world especially now, in a world where we are masked up and so socially distant. Gen Alpha, or children born after 2010, are going to be unlike any of their predecessors, especially now, thanks to the pandemic.

Many of them will lack social interaction which is so necessary during the formative years, but they will witness resilience and positivity created by bonding with their family.

This generation is being parented primarily by Millennials. The majority have a digital presence starting at birth and have had their names on social media or even have their own social accounts set up for them. The impact of not knowing true privacy or anonymity is profound.

They are part of an unintentional global experiment where screens are placed in front of them as pacifiers, entertainers and educational aids. Generation Alpha have been screenagers since birth in 2010. According to HR Mom Neha and Banker Mom Poorva, Customize parenting, according to your child need and family circumstances is the best approach you may opt as modern mom.

Gen Alpha children have adapted to technology since birth, and now they're helping their grandparents and parents adapt to it. As your child helps her grandmother or grandfather transfer her photos to the cloud or teaches them how to video call, they are growing their own self-esteem. This will serve them well as they grow up, and they will be eager to adapt to new things.

Gen Alpha don't have the same respect for hierarchies or traditional power. This isn't to say, they don't respect authority. They just have a different experience with how power can be exercised. One person on Twitter can be heard by just as many people as the president on national TV. Children in Gen Alpha know the importance, if anyone has the power, their voice will be heard.

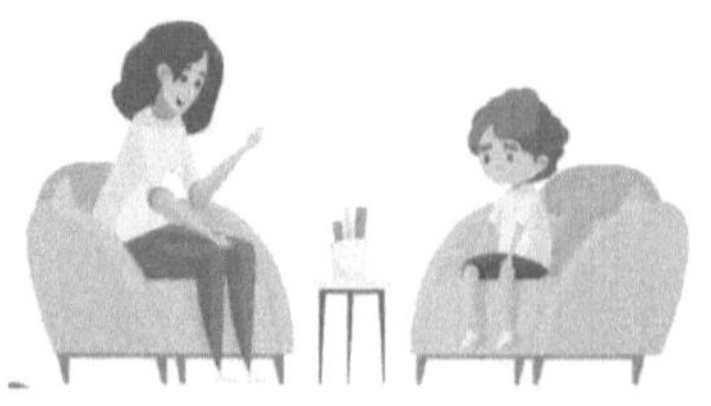

26 | What Do They Want to Say to Us?

Children Are Working Hard To Communicate With Us Through Their Behavior

It's important when we see or perceive children as "behaving badly" that we listen underneath their behavior because that's where the real information lies.

Children reflect the family system in which they are developing. A child's behavior is his amazing persistent attempt to tell us what he's feeling, what's wrong and what he needs. Children want us to know what's going on inside and to help them with it without them having to ask for their needs to be met. Their "behavior" is also giving us great information about their family system if we know how to listen.

Children often tell us how they feel by giving us the experience of what they are feeling: they convey this to us through their behavior so that we can get a felt sense of what they need us to know.

Our job is to get what is being communicated and to decide in an adult manner how we want to respond in their best interests. To do this, we must present and parent from our adult selves because it's only from there that we can understand our children are a product of our family system.

They are also having their own experiences and have imprints that may need to be heard and supported that can affect behavior too.

Children need parents to be consistently in charge and meet their needs without being asked because this creates a secure attachment. Parents need to know how to listen to their real needs and meet them proactively to prevent alpha dynamics and nourish secure attachment.

27 | Things Should be Avoided as Moms

According to new Gen imperfect Moms, We should take care of our child's individuality; we should make amendments to our daily routine and style of parenting with a few given tips:

Things we should avoid	
	Disregarding Diversity
	Lecture or Nag
	React with frustration
	Argue
	Hit, shame, or verbally abuse their child
	Over-reliance on Technology
	Comparing to Other
	Neglecting Emotional Connection
	Neglecting Real-world Skills
	Underestimating Independence
	Lack of Boundaries
	Ignoring Mental Health
	Over-scheduling
	Ignoring Environmental Concerns

Disregarding Diversity - Don't overlook the importance of teaching your child about diversity, inclusivity, and empathy towards people from different backgrounds, cultures, and perspectives.

- **Lecture or Nag** – This shattered their confidence. Try to use 25% less words.

- **React with frustration** -This leads to anxiety and depression among children.

- **Argue** – Either with the child or with a co-parent in front of their child.

- **Hit, shame, or verbally abuse their child** – This is not acceptable; the child should be handled with care and love.

- **Over-reliance on Technology** - Avoid excessive screen time and reliance on digital devices, as it can hinder social interaction, physical activity, and cognitive development.

- **Comparing to Others** - Avoid comparing your child to others or setting unrealistic expectations based on external benchmarks. Instead, focus on their individual strengths, interests, and growth.

- **Neglecting Emotional Connection** - Don't underestimate the importance of emotional connection and bonding with your child. Take time to listen, empathies, and nurture a strong emotional bond.

- **Neglecting Real-world Skills** – I believe, "Don't solely focus on academic achievement at the expense of developing practical life skills such as problem-solving, communication, and financial literacy."

- **Underestimating Independence** - Avoid overprotecting your child or micromanaging their every move. Allow them to take age-appropriate risks, make mistakes, and learn from their experiences.

- **Lack of Boundaries** - Avoid being too permissive or too authoritarian. Establish clear and consistent boundaries while also allowing for flexibility and negotiation when appropriate.

- **Ignoring mental health** - Avoid dismissing or ignoring signs of mental health issues such as anxiety, depression, or stress. Provide a supportive environment where children feel comfortable discussing their emotions and seeking help if needed.

- **Over-scheduling** – Expert mom shared, "Avoid over-scheduling your child with too many extracurricular activities, as it can lead to burnout, stress, and a lack of downtime for relaxation and creativity."

- **Ignoring Environmental Concerns** - Don't overlook the importance of environmental education and sustainability practices. Teach your child about environmental issues and encourage eco-friendly habits from an early age.

- **Manifest Faith** – Ms. Gurmeet Bindra, a full-time working mom in the healthcare field in Canada, shared valuable experiences with us. She said, "Just follow traditions, keep children in contact with grandparents and extended family. You don't have to teach or preach. Let them observe, and let them make their own connections with extended family and culture. They will simply absorb it just by being around you. You manifest faith, and they will follow it. You don't necessarily have to manifest religion or spirituality; you only manifest faith. They will spontaneously start believing in some kind of faith even if they don't understand or believe in the religion and spirituality of your roots."

Experts say, "By avoiding these pitfalls and adopting a balanced and mindful approach to parenting, you can help your child thrive and navigate the complexities of growing up in the digital age as part of Gen Z and Gen Alpha."

28 | Tips from Experts for Fellow Moms

(Invaluable 150 lessons they learned themselves in this journey of Motherhood)

Our relationship alone is what should influence a child's desire to obey, follow, attend, listen and share the same values as us, and Moms must take the lead in preserving it.

Tackling the challenges associated with Gen Z or Alpha kids requires a balanced and proactive approach that acknowledges their strengths while addressing areas where guidance and support are needed. Here are some strategies our Moms are using; you may also tailor or customize the strategies according to your child.

Deputy Registrar Mom, Ms. Suman Vashistha, explained, "There is no perfect mom, but there are plenty of things you can do that will make you a fantastic one."

1. **Find the beauty in Imperfections**: There is beauty in imperfections. You don't have to be perfect all the time. Sometimes, I would insist that I should take over a task simply because I think that I could bring the best results – at home or at work. Let me give you a little advice. Learn to let go. Delegate. Don't insist on doing everything yourself simply because you think that you can do it better. Train your support system at

home – your husband, elder children, your colleagues or subordinates at work. Let them help you, and who knows, you might be pleasantly surprised by the results.

2. **Trust Yourself** - No one knows your child better than you. Follow your instincts when it comes to their health and well-being. If you think something's wrong, chances are you're right.

3. **Be a Good Role Model** - Kids learn by watching their parents. Modelling appropriate, respectful, good behavior works much better than telling them what to do.

4. **Teach Gratitude** - Explain to your kids why values are important. The simple answer: When your kind, generous, honest, and respectful, you make the people around you feel good. More important, you feel good about yourself.

5. **Spend Quality Time With Your Kids** - Let your child choose an activity where you hang out together for 10 or 15 minutes with no interruptions. There's no better way for you to show your love.

6. **Set Limits** - Children crave limits, which help them understand and manage an often-confusing world. Show your love by setting boundaries so your kids can explore and discover their passions safely.

7. **Teach your kids social skills** - The art of conversation is an important social skill, but parents often neglect to teach it. Get a kid going with questions like, "What was your favorite part of school today?" "What did you do at the party you went to?" or "Where do you want to go tomorrow?

8. **Make Meal Time Family Time** - Sitting down at the table together is a relaxed way for everyone to connect—a time to share the happy news, talk about the day or tell a silly joke. It also helps your kids develop healthy eating habits.

9. **Praise Your Kids** - Instead of simply saying, "You're great," try to be specific about what your child did to deserve the positive feedback. When you notice your child doing something helpful or nice, let them know how you feel. It's a great way to reinforce good behavior, so they're more likely to keep doing it.

10. **Say "I love You"** - Say "I love you" whenever you feel it, even if it's 100 times a day.

    Prof. Mom Jyoti Rana explained, "Despite the challenges, my journey as a working mother has been filled with invaluable lessons and insights that I am grateful to have learned along the way." Through trial and error, I've discovered a few key tips that have helped me navigate the complexities of balancing work and motherhood:

11. **Prioritizing Self-care** – It has been essential in maintaining my physical, emotional, and mental well-being. Whether it's taking time for myself to indulge in writing poetry or practicing mindfulness, prioritizing self-care has been crucial in preventing burnout and maintaining a healthy work-life balance.

12. **Setting Boundaries** – between work and family time has been instrumental in maintaining harmony in my life. Communicating my availability to colleagues and clients and establishing clear boundaries around work hours has allowed me to be present and engaged with my children when I'm with them, without the constant distraction of work-related stressors.

13. **Seeking support** – from my partner, family members, and friends has been invaluable in navigating the challenges of working motherhood. From sharing childcare responsibilities to providing emotional support and encouragement, leaning on my support network has helped alleviate the burden of trying to do it all on my own.

14. **Recognizing that it's okay to make mistakes** – and to ask for help, and to priorities my own well-being has allowed me to embrace the messiness of life with grace and compassion.

15. **Being Present** – I try to be fully engaged with my children during the time we have together, which has been a guiding principle in my journey as a working mother. Whether it's playing games, reading stories, or simply enjoying each other's company, making the most of the time we have together has been a priority, allowing me to create lasting memories and deepen our bond.

    Dr. Renu Chaudhary also said, "Plan time to relax individually for you and spare time for the family. Make it part of your schedule to have a little alone time for yourself and some family time to have fun and chill."

16. **Celebrating My Achievements** – I celebrate my both big and small achievements with them, it has been essential in maintaining a positive mindset and acknowledging my own strength and resilience. From overcoming challenges at work to navigating the ups and downs of motherhood, celebrating my successes has been a powerful reminder of my own capabilities and the value of my contributions.

    On a final note, she added, "My journey as a working mother has been a testament to the resilience, strength, and determination of women everywhere who strive to balance multiple roles and responsibilities. And as I continue on this journey, I am grateful for the opportunity to share my experiences, insights, and reflections with fellow mothers who may be walking a similar path, knowing that together, we are stronger."

As we discussed with our next expert **Prof. Mom Amarjeet Kaur**, who is handling two young adults belonging to Gen Z, shared her experience and said, "It is a great feeling to reflect upon the time I had spent in raising my kids (a daughter and a son) especially when both of them have grown up as best human beings and doing pretty well in their respective lives." She gave amazing tips:

17. **Walk The Talk** - Live by example or in other words 'walk the talk.' Don't make any false promises to your kids which you cannot fulfil. If they see you working hard, working sincerely for them and the family, managing time effectively, respecting elders, maintaining your social life well then they will automatically adopt these virtues by observations, which are the best thing any mother can do to her kids.

18. **Be Sure About Your Priority** - Accept that priority changes based on the circumstances we are in. But, at all times, make kids feel that they were, are and will remain your priority and be actually available to them when they need you. This will gradually develop a strong reliability factor in the minds of your kids.

19. **Never give up on 'Me Time,' Self-care, Self-love and Self-respect** - While understanding the difference between self-centered and self-care. If you love yourself, that will automatically get transmitted to your kids and will ultimately help them learn the importance of self-care and self-respect.

20. **Don't Get Pray To Social Pressures** - like: how come you get time to walk every day; how could you manage time to watch a movie with your partner or go on a date with him; how could you continue with your 8 hours job while leaving kids with your in-laws or maid; how did you not accompany your kid to a competition etc. Remember that your circumstances are peculiar to you, and others may not know what is going on in your life.

21. **Don't Neglect Your Social Life and Life with Your Partner** - Believe me or not, it is possible to spend time with

your family and friends while taking good care of your kids. In fact, it helps them learn social skills from childhood itself.

22. **Allow them to Grow Gracefully without Defining many Rules and Restrictions** - Remember that kids grow very fast and their needs change in different phases of their lives, and so does your importance and need to them. Accept this fact gracefully and allow them to grow without defining many rules and restrictions on them. This will develop a trust factor between you and your kids and strengthen your bond.

23. **Make your kids part of Decision Making** - When they gain some sense, of course, while keeping an eye that there could be some mistakes but no blunder. It could begin with a smallest of the small decision of allowing them to order food in a restaurant when you all are dining out to allow them to choose their dress and may lead to big decisions like choosing their career, their partner etc.

24. **Re-iterate Virtues, Facts and Actions** - Always re-iterate those virtues, facts and actions which you think are important for quality life based on your outlook on life. For example, I have mentioned, maybe a thousand times to my kids to spend time and money on (i) health, (ii) good food, (iii) relations, (iv) education and (v) travelling/experiences in this very descending order and have never let any chance go to prove the same. It has helped them to come up as individuals who know their priorities.

While concluding, she said, "The hardest part of being a mother is that we are expected to be all sorted out: no mistakes, no grudges, no tiredness, no complaints etc. However, motherhood doesn't come with a user's handbook, and if we listen to our hearts honestly and follow our intuitions, we can never go wrong. The reason being, only those people can intuit fairly well who are sensitive to their own emotions, own needs and that of emotions and needs of others too, which include your kids too."

Dr. Renu Chaudhary further expanded the topic and said,

25. **Setting up a Schedule** The most important thing is that you have to spend extra time setting up a schedule. Things will flow a lot better for everyone if you have predictable routines that are visible to you and your partner and kids.

26. **Don't try to be a Perfectionist** – Don't compete with your near and dear.

27. **Keep Things Simple** that really work for you.

28. **Balance is the Key Mantra** – She said, "I tried to balance my life as much as possible. No extremes on either end. If you feel like you can't keep it up, figure out how you can modify the situation."

29. **Feel Proud of Yourself to be a mother** it's a God Gift. You don't need a certificate of perfectionist. You already know what is best for your kid and for yourself, stick to your instincts.

Prof. Mom Meenakshi Sheoran is handling two generations together. One is a young adult, whereas the other belongs to Gen Alpha; both girls and boys have different choices and different needs; here are some tips she would like to share with us:

30. **Essential Quality time**- Prof. Meenakshi suggested, "Either morning five min or evening 5 minutes spend quality time with them. Mothers need everything according to themselves but sometime they don't require a perfect mom but a mom who is listening to them."

31. **Don't lie in front of them** - What may the situation is, never ever lie otherwise in future you have to face the consequences.

32. **Gender sensitization** – She explained, "Gender sensitization involves raising awareness and understanding about gender equality and the issues surrounding gender identity, roles, and stereotypes. Gender sensitization is essential for fostering both girls - boys and the society where everyone can thrive regardless of their gender identity and establish neutral gender."

33. **Don't label Child** - This generation is full of questions, they are curious to know everything and When we are short of answers we just tell them to keep quite or label them as difficult child but it's not right. May be because of our upbringing and conditioning we can't resonate with them but they have their own answers to every question, just give them space and facilities so they may thrive.

34. **Don't judge and increase your listening capacity** – Because they want to be heard and understand their point of view, maybe we can learn something new from them.

35. **Establish clear and consistent rules** – Establishing clear rules and limits around screen time, online activities, and technology use to ensure a healthy balance between digital and offline activities. Establish clear and consistent rules and boundaries regarding behavior, responsibilities and technology use. Communicate these boundaries effectively and enforce them fairly.

36. **Providing Guidance** – Offering guidance and support to help children navigate the digital world safely, teaching them about online safety, privacy, and responsible internet use.

37. **Encouraging Critical Thinking** – Promoting critical thinking skills to help children evaluate information and media critically, discerning between reliable sources and misinformation online.

38. **Modelling Behavior** – Serving as positive role models by demonstrating healthy tech habits, managing their own screen time, and engaging in meaningful offline activities with their children.

39. **Fostering Communication** – Creating open lines of communication where children feel comfortable discussing their online experiences, concerns, and questions with their parents or caregivers.

40. **Encourage Independence** – Provide opportunities for alpha kids to make decisions, solve problems, and take on responsibilities appropriate for their age and maturity level. Encourage autonomy while offering guidance and support as needed.

41. **Channel Their Energy Positively** – alpha kids often have a lot of energy and drive. Encourage them to channel this energy into productive and constructive activities such as sports, creative pursuits, or community involvement.

42. **Teach Social Skills** – Help alpha kids develop strong interpersonal skills, including active listening, empathy, and conflict resolution. Encourage positive social interactions and provide opportunities for them to practice these skills.

43. **Promote Emotional Intelligence** – Teach alpha kids to recognise and manage their emotions effectively. Encourage open communication about feelings and provide support and guidance in navigating difficult emotions and situations.

44. **Provide Structure and Routine Establish a predictable daily routine** with consistent meal times, bedtime, and homework schedules. Structure helps alpha kids feel secure and provides a framework for their day.

45. **Foster a Growth Mindset** – Encourage a positive attitude towards learning and growth. Teach alpha kids that mistakes

are opportunities for learning and improvement and that success comes through effort and perseverance.

46. **Stay Calm in Hectic or Emotional Situations** – Social Worker and Homemaker Madhu Sharma gave us the golden rule "Stay Calm" yes calmness is the best way to avoid anxiety and depression.

47. **Stand by your child in any situation** - She said, "Regardless of age group, give your full support and empathy to your child. If the whole world is still against him/ her, if they have your full support, they can reach the stars. You are their biggest support."

48. **Think flexibly and go with the flow** – She said, "If plan A doesn't work for you, just move on to plan B, then C, then D and so on." "Never lose hope" She further elaborated "If you lose by heart, you can never win the battel but if you are strong enough to face the situation and try your best, no one in the world can stop you to achieve your goals."

49. **Known-Seen-Heard** – Germany-based NRI Ruchi says, "Give your child the sense of feeling 'known, seen and heard' – listen with your eyes, ears and heart (not with cell phone in hand)."

50. **Lead by Example** – Model the behaviors and values you want to instill in alpha kids, including resilience, responsibility, and respect for others. Be mindful of your own reactions and attitudes, as children often learn by example.

51. **Seek Professional Support if Needed** – Investment Banker Mom Palak Kalra said, "If alpha kids are struggling with significant behavioral or emotional challenges, don't hesitate to seek support from a qualified therapist, counsellor, or mental health professional."

52. **Foster With Love and Care** – She further said, "Staying in the lead means inviting the dominant child to depend on us.

We cannot force a child to rest in our care, but we can work to create the conditions that will foster it by accepting the work of the relationship and assuming the alpha role in the child's life."

53. **Remove Anger in Different Way** – HR Neha said, "If your child no longer cries, set limits in order that the child hits the 'wall of futility' and then be able to hold a calm space for the inevitable temper tantrums which will hopefully be accompanied by tears – this is adaptive and the goal."

54. **Delegate and Take Help** – HR Divya Arora said, "Life will anyhow move on, it will never stop, you have to manage everything within the timeline, and you are not an alien with ten hands, so be relaxed and take help from other, delegate work to your family members or house help. It may look weird to you, but believe me; it will give you more relief in terms of prioritizing your work and the things which matter the most."

55. **Never Take Too much Stress to be Perfect** – Homemaker Madhu Sharma said, "The Joy of living with imperfections gives you satisfaction, life will never be easy, ups and downs are part of life, just be true to yourself and to your love once, the universe has to give you what you deserve. So, Don't try to be perfect, just be True."

56. **Repair and Protect The Relation** – Centre Head Sushma Sharma gave us a golden tip for handling teenagers, "To accept the work of the relationship is to keep our finger on the pulse of whether our children feel close to us, depend on us, and trust us. If our relationship feels strained on weakened, we need to repair and protect it and refrain from using separation-based discipline methods."

57. **Play with your child and really immerse yourself in their world** – She said, "If they can't come to you, just go to them. Tell them you are the most amazing thing that happened

to us. Now the time has changed; rather than assuming and silently watching everything, it's time to react."

58. **Be their anchor, be their compass** – Yes, you, my dear fellow Moms; it's the key to a good relationship.

59. **Give them hugs and kisses -** Tell them how important you (child) are in their lives. Hug them, kiss them as often as you can; this will create wonders.

60. **Find ways to connect meaningful relationships** – Nobody wants to be in a relationship where only one person is dominating the other. Equality is the key factor. As they grow up, teenagers give them the power to choose and share feelings. Not the authority in you but equal opportunity to flourish.

61. **Be The Compass** – Asst. Manager Priyanka Tanwar said, "To claim an alpha role in a child's life is to act as their compass point and to help them make sense of the world around them. It means we don't simply meet their demands but anticipate their needs, and we seize the lead in nurturing and comforting them when they are facing futilities that are part of life."

62. **Be The In charge** – She further explain, "To invite a child to rest in our care we need to portray a strong alpha presence so that they feel we are in charge and can handle whatever comes our way, from tantrums, to resistance, to emotional outbursts."

63. **Create a safe space for their child to express their feelings -** HR Neha said, "It's really important to create a safe place for your child; make it a habit to give your time to listen to their imaginative stories; this is how you may understand, what's there in their mind. Never let your child unlistened."

64. **Learn to Say "No"** – She also said, "Now the time has changed. No means No & it's true & if you are not feeling comfortable in something or you don't want to give energy to

someone else, it's better to say No; it's better to give yourself priority on everyone else, for you, your family and most importantly your child's betterment."

65. **Get to know your kids** - **Entrepreneur Alka** said, "Watch how they approach play and what interests them. That will help you know how best to show them they are safe and loved during those tough toddler moments. At the initial age, your child is everything. Sometimes, you have to leave your career or ladies, u can take a break from your work temporarily; later, you may rejoin it just like I did."

66. **Setting priority – Mom Blogger and Software Engineer Prachi** also agree with this and said, "It was not that easy for me to do things while living in joint family setup. But somehow you have to set the priorities and do things which you are passionate about."

67. **Time management** – She said, "As I am becoming active and doing time management very nicely, credit goes to my son, obviously."

68. **Reading motivational stories together** - we have started reading the story books at bedtime. Stories of gods, Ramayana, which I started story-telling to him.

69. **Be his best friend** - and by giving him freedom to express his feelings rather than imposing my feelings. Try to motivate him on little things by praising him for his little and celebrating.

70. **Brushing your skill & prepare yourself for second inning -** Software Engineer Prachi shared, "I somehow kept on brushing my skills so that I can easily step into the job once I start giving interviews. And slowly and gradually I was able to restart my career."

71. **Communicating things clearly beforehand** – She said, "I practice this so that he gets mentally prepared for things we

are introducing or any transition that is coming into his life. I start preparing his mind in advance slowly and gradually."

72. **Play family games & enjoy vocations together** - As a family, we go out on vacations and in the name of activity, we play games like Cricket, badminton, UNO Cards, and Carrom board.

73. **Control the Extra Pampering** - To avoid taking extra advantage, grandparents even take the initiative to control any kind of wrong behavior.

74. **Socialization from Early Age** - Prachi shared, "My son and I are both social and today, I also remember the day when I took him to the nearby garden in the stroller when he was eight months old. From that time, he has always gone for evening walks, and he is very social and likes to talk to everyone around and crack jokes to make other kids laugh. I also take him to the club to play lawn tennis, where he gets an opportunity to focus on the game and socialize as well. Recently, I joined the Mom & Kids Club, 'Momzilla,' so that he could socialize with other kids, and it brought a smile to his face. We want to learn and grow together."

75. **Don't Spoon-feed** – Yes, this is really important. "Stop paying attention to spoon-feeding him and asking him to complete the H.W.H.W. Today is when he is independent and takes out his how to complete and not on his head every time like a helicopter to tell him to do this and do that. Now, he is more worried than me about his H.W.H.W., timetable, stationery and everything."

76. **Stop over explaining everyone** - You should set some boundaries and give proper answers in which you can simply say that It's my own decision and I don't want to give any explanation further.

77. **Cuddle Your Little Munchkins** - Dr. Shelly suggested, "If you have small kids, please cuddle them more, listen to their stories, and spend quality time together."

78. **More of mutual discussion then advise** – She further explain, Teenagers and young adults should be treated with care and try to understand their point of view also we should more open to career choices.

79. **Undivided Attention** - It's the biggest thing you can give to your child, Just you and your little one.

80. **Self-care is important**. If you keep yourself healthy, fit, and fine, your kids will also learn the importance of self-love.

81. **Home No Phone Zone** - Keep your phone off when they talk, try to maintain your home No phone zone, I know it's not possible all the time but for few hours this regime can be maintained.

82. **Listen to their stories** - When they return from school or from somewhere just listen their experience and stories, these are the memories you are creating for yourself.

83. **Never let anyone abuse you or your child** – They listen to everything, they observe everything, they remember everything, just take care of their innocence.

84. **Be Patient Listener** - They do not always want advice, just be a patient listener. Sometime listening without any solution or advice, is all they want.

85. **No need to pressurize children** - **Homemaker Swati Mittal** advice to new mothers, "There is no need to pressurize the children. They need their own pace to do their things. Every child is blessed with some qualities and marks in the school really doesn't matter in future life. Life can take turn at any time."

86. **Avoid Micro Management** - Today's parents are much educated and aware, they are too much caring but I think this micro management is not good for children.

87. **Avoid Emphasize Your Mindset on them** – She shared, "I try to understand their feelings, give them the space they need and don't emphasize my mindset on them."

88. **Develop Understanding** – With time, as the children grow, mothers should be more understanding. We should try to make our children independent and let them do their own things in their own way.

89. **Communication is the key to a healthy relationship** - H.R.H.R. Mom Neha said, "Communication play in maintaining a healthy and open relationship with your child is very important and required in today's time."

90. **Foster independence and resilience** -She further explained, "Foster independence and resilience in your child, knowing they won't have siblings to lean on is crucial, but I always try to communicate with her and show her worth is way more important, and she can touch the stars all alone."

91. **Alone can-do wonders** - Educator Sana Inamdar said, I always tell my son how capable he is in all aspects, and also he can do things alone without any sibling.

92. **Never fear of challenges** – She said, "Never fear of challenges, always talk to you child, see their area of interest, do good thing in front of them so they will observe you and learn from that."

93. **They don't need a friend more than you – She further advice, "manage your time, talk to them, play with them, don't make them feel they need a friend more then you."**

94. **Don't make your child's achievements your prestige issue – Homemaker Lippi Gulati** gave advice to all the

Moms, "Don't make your child's achievements your prestige issue. Every child has his/her own pace."

95. **Listen to their opinion and treat them as individuals** - As we are getting older the bond with my adult children is getting stronger. I do this while listening to their opinions and treating them as an individual that they are.

96. **Enjoy Evolving Journey** - The role of motherhood keeps on changing as the children grow as adults; Lippi said, "The role reverses as they grow older; instead of taking advice now, they are my consultant."

97. **Provide Opportunities for Socialization -** Delhi-based Centre head Mom Sushma Sharma said, "Interaction with peers for your child is way more important" As my both the daughters are in their teenage so I try to take them in Social gatherings or at least visiting their cousins home once a month.

98. **Plan Entire Day - Homemaker Hema Sharma** explained, "Make a to-do list and finish all work in a timely manner & try to spend enough time. So, They feel that I am always with them. I try to do their favorite activities- park, arts & crafts, gardening, swimming & to listen to bedtime stories."

99. **Develop Positive Approach** – She suggested, "Always important to understand child's behavior first, then we can learn to develop positive approach."

100. **Same Time Same Activity** – She said, "While managing two alphas together, I try to plan their activity smartly e.g., Same time same work like sketching, drawing, playing, studies etc. Through this they learn the basics of sibling attitude like sharing and supporting each other."

101. **Strategically Enhance Self Confidence** – She explained, "I give only 'small task to complete' they try to complete that with problem-solving skills. It helps to increase – The Self Confidence."

102. Appreciate Their Small Achievements – This leads to bigger ones and simultaneously teaches them not to overreact.

103. Teach them to Give Respect and Get Respect – She disclose the secret tip, "I always tell them to give respect and get that in return, never ever disrespect even though they are servants or younger than us."

104. Time is the most precious thing – Homemaker Mrs. Mittal suggested to all the young Moms, "Give your precious tiny miracles the most important thing in world, time; never let your child feel your absence and left no mark being perfect."

105. Handle with Love and Care – Educator in special education Seema Arora said, "Whether you have a normal child or special child, feel their emotions and handle them with care."

106. Recognise their hidden Talent – She further explain, "Every child is unique in his own way, you just need to find out their passion and ability, just like I did, Although he comes under special child category but he is amazing With the wheels of confidence and wings of creativity he has learned piano, tabla and basketball, he loves singing with me, I feel blessed with his presence in my life."

107. Create a Supportive System – She suggested, "You can't do everything alone, so be practical and be open for giving and taking help."

108. Positive Parenting – She said, "There is something good in everything, whether you accept or not. If you keep everything simple and positive, God will help you achieve your and your family's dreams."

109. Understand their needs and let him understand yours – Entrepreneur Samiksha Bharadwaj shared her trick, "I always keep my son's needs and priority first. I spend time with him or talk about his interests, and then I share my interests so that he can understand. I had to apply time management. And I also teach him to be independent and do small tasks on his own."

110. **Daily Hug** – Believe me, Moms, It's a Magic…… Keep doing magic every day.

111. **No Comparison with others** - Moms, please never ever compare your child with anyone because I believe everyone is unique.

112. **Become your child's best friend** – She suggested, "Make your connection strong. I always try to listen his word then We work together on a solution that doesn't involve invalidating my child's emotions."

113. **Teach him the importance of self-care** – It is important to teach him how important self-care is, it's not selfishness it's all about grooming and try to create an impact, feel good factor boost self-confidence.

114. **Encourage To Ask Questions** – She explained, "Curiosity is the key factor of learning and developing mind growth. Encourage him to clarify your doubts with teacher, friends, family members without any hesitation."

115. **Advice for Mom with a single child** - Having single child is your decision. But make a best relationship with your kids. So that they feel safe and connected with world and they enjoy their life.

116. **Make them Independent** – Try to make them independent in their growing age itself. There are two things Moms should give their children: roots and wings.

117. **Leftover everything for child's need** – Banker Mom Poorva Chaturvedi said, "One thing at a time. I left over everything besides, in my opinion, my child's childhood is precious however we are living in a digital era so I believe I can restart career and my personal interest at any time or I can say at any age."

118. **Ignore trolls**, whether they are from family or outside.

119. **Do not expect anything from anyone** - Feel positive within also motivate yourself every day and do not expect anything from anyone other than family members, expectation leads to disappointment.

120. **Keep an eye of what they are watching** – Student Counsellor Deepika said, "It's a digital world you can't control them to use these things but you can keep an eye on them and navigate them to use their time effectively."

121. **Mindfulness & positive parenting** - Architect and Midbrain Educator Anu Bansal shared, "Mindfulness is the key to achieving success in life."

122. **Brain Gym, Meditation and Yoga** – She further elaborated, "Activating midbrain through these techniques gives you wings to acquire and adapt knowledge."

123. **Don't Raise Them Like Cattles** – Phonics and Spoken English Coach Suman Agarwal said, "SPEND QUALITY TIME WITH YOUR CHILDREN. UNDERSTAND THEIR STATE OF MIND. DON'T RAISE THEM AS WE RAISE CATTLE. BE WISER, ACT WISER, THEY ONLY NEED YOUR POSITIVE NUDGING."

124. **Don't Burden Them with Future Expectations** – She suggested, "I TRY TO READ THEIR MINDS. I ALLOW THEM TO FEEL THEIR FEELINGS. I DON'T BURDEN THEM WITH ANY EXPECTATIONS FOR FUTURE."

125. **Education and Confidence** – Homemaker Ms. Shashi Jain, who belongs to Generation X, guided us through the timeline and suggested, "Inculcating the value of Education and confidence from an early age takes them to success at any age," she elaborated, "Rather than giving dowry give them these powerful weapons to fight any battles of future."

126. **Creating the Bonding between Siblings** – She said beautifully, "Mother is the source of creating amazing bonding

between siblings, Put your heart and soul to crate this lifelong friendship."

127. **Trust Them in Any Situation –** She said, "No matter what, stand by your child, regardless of any age or gender. If you do not support them, who else will." Be the backbone of their life, be the comfort zone of any problem, Be their light, Be their fight, Be there everything.

128. **Love Is The Best Discipline** – Working mom Gurmeet Bindra from Canada shared a valuable tip with us. She has been enjoying her motherhood journey for the last 23 years. With her experience, she elaborated, "Love is the best discipline." Whatever attributes and good habits you can instigate with love will stay with your child for his whole life. If you discipline your child with force, you will only get temporary results. To raise a strong character and a person with strong integrity, you have to be soft and persistent, not strict and demanding.

129. **Meet their needs instead of their demands** -Homemaker Priya Khandelwal said, "Rather than fulfilling their unnecessary demands, just focus on their needs."

130. **Stroke their back and arms as they** said cuddling is really important for a child's mental growth, so live your life to the fullest.

131. Don't court battles

132. Walk to Bed with them.

133. Bake Goodies for them and their friends.

134. Give them a massage.

135. Pick up your teenagers in the middle of the night from wherever they call you.

136. Plan activities where you are in the lead

137. Go places where they rely on you to orient them.

138.   Attach through sharing food together.

139.   When they're sick, go over the top to take care of them.

140.   When you're sick, you can still be in charge and let the child know what the plan is for the day, etc.

141. Encourage their child to express themselves through open-ended questions.

142. Understand that mistakes are inevitable and good learning experiences.

143. Encourage their child to come up with possible solutions and outcomes in difficult situations.

144. Express confidence that their child will be able to handle any situation.

145. Set reasonable expectations.

146. Plan fun and rewarding activities frequently.

147. Share stories of their successes and failures.

148. Make sure their words match their actions.

149. Remember that their child has not yet developed emotional and impulse control and that parents must model this behavior.

150. Master the Art of Organizing and Prioritizing

Note: Because of certain agreements, a few names are not mentioned and kept confidential.

In conclusion, I believe that, "Perfection is nothing just an illusion" while striving to be a "super mom" can be admirable, it's essential for Moms to priorities their own well-being and seek support when needed. Balancing multiple roles and responsibilities is challenging, and it's okay to ask for help and practice self-compassion along the way.

29 | The key is Progress, Not Perfection

The alpha Parent Model reveals a new perspective and an emotionally compelling vision of the type of parent you can be for your child. The simplicity of this model helps you get straight to the core of why you (and your child) behave the way you do.

Because relationships and life circumstances are too complex to fit neatly into any box, no real parent falls into any single category or type. Instead, I encourage parents to customize their own model and take our tips as a guide to creating your vision for what type of mom you want to be.

The key is progress, not perfection. When you have a clear and compelling vision for the type of mom you want to be and why, you can take small steps every day to make progress toward that vision.

30 | Thank You Note

First of all, I would like to say thanks to God, who looks after me. My readers, for their love & support. Universe, for abundance. All the Moms who participated in my research work; they shared their untold stories, sometimes we cried together, sometimes we laughed together, and some feelings were felt immediately, whereas @ 1 point I lost my self, remembering my hard times, overall within this journey of research work I can see myself growing, I edited the pattern which I was following as Mom.

Now as, I am standing holding this book in my hand, with loads of hope that every mom will find a bit of herself in this book. Thanks once again for helping me during my journey. Although there are many names that I want to write down because of the confidentiality agreement, I can't take their names, but the experience they shared is truly commendable. I am grateful for this opportunity, and I'll forever remember your contribution to writing this masterpiece.

I Thank my Father & Mom, Mrs Madhu Sharma, for raising us as a confident child; my whole personality is the blend of my father's calmness and my mom's courage to face every situation single-handedly. My husband Gaurav, Thanks for going above and beyond for my happiness and passion. My sons Mann and Gaurik, I really appreciate your dedication and support. My eldest sister, Mrs. Suman Vashistha, who has always remained my first reader and editor; I Couldn't have done it without you. Thank you, Di. Mrs. Sushma Sharma, Thank you for your vital role in this project. Mrs. Neha Vashistha, Thanks for your indispensable help. Aditya, I would like to enhance my knowledge with your suggestions, Mrs. Divya Arora. Your efforts didn't go unnoticed; thank you. My extended family members and friends, for your direct – indirect support and outstanding contribution, thank you from the bottom of my heart.

Thanks to the Team Secret Purple Diary and Mission Purple. Grateful for your expertise and assistance. Your input was crucial. Thank you, Prof. Jyoti Rana, Prof. Amarjeet Kaur, Dr. Renu Chaudhary, and Prof. Meenakshi Sheoran, for enhancing the value of this book with your expert advice and guidance; I am grateful.

Thank you, Club Momzilla, Mrs Chanchal Jain, Mrs Priya Khandelwal, Mrs Garima Batra, Mrs Sakshi Jain, Mrs Sakshi Batra, Mrs Bhawna Tiwari, Mrs Mohini Mahawar, Mrs Prachi Kalra, Mrs Leena Wadhwa, Mrs, Mrs Anupriya Gupta, Mrs Ekta, Mrs Radhika, Mrs Tanisha Jain, Mrs Radhika Jain, Mrs Pranjul Gupta, Mrs Gunjan Rustagi, Dr. Nidhi Jain; Your contribution made a world of difference, Thank you another family. Thanks, JK club Moms, Mrs Shashi Jain, Mrs. Mittal, Mrs Lippi Gulati, Mrs Goyal, Mrs Jain, Mrs Gupta, and Mrs Swati Mittal for your invaluable input.

- My dear friends and mentors Dr. Shelly Narula Gupta, Mrs Rajni, Mrs Poorva Chaturvedi, Mrs Samiksha Bhardwaj, Mrs Hema Sharma, Mrs Sana Inamdar, Mrs Prachi Kalra, Ms. Palak Kalra, Ruchi Di, Mrs Anu Bansal, Mrs. Seema Arora, Ms. Deepika, Mrs. Suman Agarwal, Mrs. Alka Mahawar; Grateful for the collaborative spirit your help was truly appreciated. My extended family on Instagram and Facebook. Once again, You dear reader for your tremendous support.

Thanks to all the Moms for being part of this journey and helping me directly – and indirectly; grateful for your support in completing this project – Mompedia is not only my book; it's about every single mom who is struggling from inside but smiling from outside.

Let's make this world a better place for all the perfectly – imperfect Moms like me.

Thank you! Thank you! Thank you!

About the Author

Archana Vashistha is an accomplished author whose words have the power to transport readers to new world and ignite their imaginations. She is a poet social activist, educator, content creator, founder of Allure Reads by Archana & the founder members of Mission Purple & Momzilla club. She is a true Delhiite by heart & soul.

Her second career inning has been marked by impactful initiatives like "Mission Purple," which has helped more than 1700 women & children in Delhi & NCR. Through this initiative, she is spreading awareness of & importance about mental health. She is The Purple Changemaker of our society. To emphasize the importance of mother child bond she along with few teachers started the first ever Mom & Kid's Club in her city.

Her life is a beautiful blend of creativity and family values. Her ability to craft captivating stories and nurture her two sons demonstrates her multifaceted talents and her deep commitment to both her art and her family.

To know more about her books, life & upcoming projects, visit her website, www.archanavashistha.com.

Allure Reads by Archana

Introducing the newest addition to the literary scene: the Book Review and Reading Club! Dive into the world of literature with fellow book enthusiasts as we explore captivating stories, exchange insightful reviews, and foster a community of avid readers. Join us on a journey of literary discovery and discussion like never before!

What will you find in this Mompedia?

1. Fun facts about motherhood

2. Different generations different moms

3. Why Today's Moms are different from other generations

4. How today's kids are different

5. Different Styles of parenting approaches

6. What is Society's approach

7. What are the needs of today's generation

8. How Parenting style has changed because of technology

9. What is best parenting approach

10. What kind of challenges /problems Moms are facing

11. How we can resolve the issue of generation gap

12. Solutions based on practical approach and real-life examples

13. Tips for fellow Moms

14. Best read if you are a mom, mom to be, husband, father to be or you are a kid and want to know more about you Mom

15. 1 stop solution for all the misconceptions about motherhood.

Secret
PURPLE DIARY